FROM THE PASTOR'S PEN

THE PASTORAL LETTERS OF

Fred A. Hill, Jr.

San Antonio, Texas

Printed by Kindle Direct Publishing
Publication arranged by Eremite Publishing

ISBN: 978-1-9806-0720-5

Cover design by Evan K. Kahlich

TABLE OF CONTENTS

About the Author

GOD CALLED Fred A. Hill Jr. to teach and preach the Gospel of Jesus Christ from the piney woods of East Texas. He was born on a farm just outside the sawmill town of Doucette, Texas in 1928. He is the youngest of five children born to Fred and Letha Hill. Fred Sr. was a lumber train engineer that brought logs into the Long-Bell Lumber Company mill and later ran his own sawmill.

From these woods of Tyler County, Texas, God saved, filled with the Holy Spirit and called Fred Hill Jr. to proclaim the message of Jesus. Junior began his ministry as a young man preaching revivals in Texas. In 1953 he married Betty Jane Kiff, and was sent by God on a life's journey of Christian service.

In what is now nearly seventy years of ministry, God provided avenues for powerful ministry throughout Texas, Louisiana, the midwestern states and California in revivals, campmeetings and church pastorates. Stories of God's work through their ministry abound. Many lives are touched and changed by the Holy Spirit because of their obedient service to the Lord.

Fred currently resides near Tomball, Texas with his wife Betty where they recently celebrated 65 years of marriage. Though nearing 90, "Pastor" Hill still proclaims the life-giving message that Jesus saves! There are more stories of mercy and faith yet to be told!

MIKE NESBIT
January 2018

Preface

These thought-provoking articles were originally written to be part of a weekly bulletin mailed to church members and friends. I utilized this method as a tool to minister the life-changing Word to my congregation and to anyone interested in receiving a weekly word of truth. Though first published over forty years ago, the topics and themes of the Bible-based messages remain vitally relevant today.

Included in this collection is my article on tribulation instructions first written and published in 1982. The instructions are based chiefly on the New Testament book of Revelation and many key scripture passages are included. Though my purposes in 1982 and today remain the same, there is a great sense of urgency to renew the proclamation of this Bible teaching.

I encourage you to read and reflect on the articles with an open heart and ear to hear what the Holy Spirit will say to you today. I believe you will find His life-giving truth. Through faith in God, act on that truth and you will find His joy and victory in every circumstance and situation you face!

PASTOR FRED A. HILL

The Bible: The Miracle Book

> For the prophecy came not in old time by the will
> of man: but holy men of God spake as they were
> moved by the Holy Ghost.
>
> 2 PETER 1:21

Every time you pick up the Bible, you pick up a
miracle, for the Bible is a miracle of oneness, unity
and harmony. It is a library of 66 books—if you
divide the Psalms into five books, as they possibly
should be, you would have 70, which is God's perfect
number, 7 times 10, the number of completion or
fulfillment—written by 35 different authors, in a
period of approximately 1500 years. Represented in
the authors is a cross section of humanity, educated
and uneducated, including kings, fishermen, public
officials, farmers, teachers and physicians. Some of
the subjects included are religion, history, law, science,
poetry, drama, biography and prophecy.

For 35 authors with such varied religious,
educational and economic backgrounds to unite on so
many subjects, harmoniously, and over a period of
1500 years, is a miracle that can only be explained by
2 Peter 1:21 and 2 Timothy 3:16. "All Scripture is
given by inspiration of God." The word "inspiration"
means "God-breathed." So this accounts for the
miracle of unity and harmony of the Bible; while it

was written by some 35 different men, it actually has only *one* author: God!

Some have said that the Bible lacks style, that it doesn't flow as a book should, that it lacks depth and its phraseology and composition is poor. But this is man's opinion and again, we say God did not write to speak to man's intellect, but to his heart.

The simplicity of the Scripture is what makes it so forceful. You may not understand Daniel's prophecy or Revelation, but you can understand John 3:3 and Romans 3:23. It is not what man doesn't understand about the Bible that really bothers him, rather it is what he *does* understand that disturbs him.

The Bible: Our Source of Light

Thy word is a lamp unto my feet and a *light* unto my path.
PSALM 119:105

The ancients had little lamps that fastened to the toes of their sandals, and as they walked, these little lamps cast their light upon the pathway, thus the reason for the psalmist's remarks concerning the Word of God. The lighted pathway is the *exclusive privilege* of the child of God. The Scripture is very plain in revealing this truth for we walk not in darkness (not that there is no darkness) and we are children of the *day* (or *light*) and not of the night. There is no darkness and no night for the Christian because we have the eternal light of God's Word.

The Bible, our source of light, is a far greater light than the candle, for it does not burn away or the wind cannot blow it out. It is a far greater light than the old kerosene lamp that often smoked up the globe or ran low on kerosene and had to be shaken to get a few minutes more light. The Bible never runs out of oil. It is far greater than the flashlight, for it doesn't dim with use or corrode away, but the more you use the Bible, the brighter it becomes. It is far greater than our electric lights, for no storm can ever interrupt its power to produce light; in fact, it gives more light in the midst of the storm. The Bible is a far greater source of light than the sun, for the sun shines on only half the world at a time, but we who have the Word never have to wait in the cold night for Bible light, for we *walk not* in darkness.

And who has greater vision than the Bible believer? No one! We see not only the present, but we can also see into the glorious future. What unbeliever would dare say what he will be doing a thousand years from now? But we who believe know *what* we will be doing and *where* we will be living, praise God! Not only can we see the future, but we, through the light of the Bible, can also see the past. All the way back to the Fall of Man and further. . . . Let the light shine, oh Lord! Let it shine on our terrible past that we may see clearly any ugly sinful thing that is not covered by the blood of Jesus that we may repent and pray until it is gone, buried, removed and forgotten, washed away not by the flood, but by the blood.

"But if we *walk* in the *light, as He is in the light,* we have fellowship one with another, and the blood of Jesus Christ, His Son, cleanseth from all sin."

The Bible: The Sword of the Spirit

And take the helmet of salvation, and the sword of the Spirit, which is the word of God.

EPHESIANS 6:17

What a weapon the Word of God is! Hebrews 4:12 says the Word is quick (active) and powerful and sharper than *any* two-edged sword, piercing even to the diving asunder (piercing through the body and laying open the innermost recesses of the soul and mind) of the soul and spirit, and of the joints and marrow, and is a discerner of the thoughts and intent of the heart.

Paul writes in 2 Corinthians 3:6 these words: "The letter killeth, but the spirit giveth life." Remember the Bible is the sword of the Spirit. It is not your weapon, but rather, it is the Spirit's weapon. When we try to handle the Word of God without the unction of the Spirit (in witnessing, teaching, preaching) we are about as successful as *a brain surgeon operating blindfolded.* We have a sharp and powerful instrument but not the eyes or sense of direction of the Spirit to guide us in the use of it. We may be able to cut others down with the Word, but it brings only death and disappointment when we lack the anointing.

Pray! Pray until you get the unction of the Holy Spirit upon your life, then the Word will become a new instrument in your life for the Holy Spirit will use you and the Word to bring life, joy, and peace to others.

Remember! God put a flaming sword to keep man from the tree of life in the garden (Gen. 3:24) after man fell. This flaming sword would have produced sudden death, no doubt. But God gave us the living Word, the sword of the Spirit —flaming with truth, not to keep us *from,* but to point us *to* Jesus, who gives unto those who believe "eternal life."

The Bible: Soul Food

> Man doth not live by bread only, but by every word
> that proceedeth out of the mouth of the Lord doth
> man live.
>
> DEUTERONOMY 8:3

There is overwhelming evidence in the Word
and also in the lives of men that the Bible is
certainly food for the soul of man. The psalmist
writes in Psalm 119:103: "How sweet are thy
words; yea, sweeter than honey." Peter spoke of
"desiring the sincere milk of the Word, that ye
may grow thereby," and Paul writes of feeding
with the milk of the Word because they were not
mature enough to take the *strong* meat of the
Scripture. While these Scripture references point
to the fact that the Bible is "soul food," let us
also look at ourselves. The leanness of the soul
or spiritual life of any person can simply be laid
to the fact that he or she doesn't eat of the
Word. Perhaps there is a "lack of appetite" for
the Bible. If there is, then purpose in your heart
to read so many chapters each day until the
Word becomes to you the same as it was to the
psalmist—"sweeter than honey."

There is *no* excuse for any Christian being
lean and barren in his soul. There is *no* excuse
for spiritual immaturity or childishness. The
Christian who pouts when he doesn't have his

way, or takes his ball and goes home unless one plays by his rules, needs to feed upon the Word so he can grow up and grow out of such childishness.

Now just because the Word is preached from the pulpit doesn't mean that you're spiritually hale and hearty. There is a lot of malnutrition in America today, though there is an abundance of good nutritional food. The minister may spread an excellent table filled with heavenly manna of God's Word, but people must do more than just "come," they must also "dine."

We Have This Treasure

But we have this treasure in earthen vessels, that the excellency of the power may be of God, and not of us.

2 CORINTHIANS 4:7

One thing that fails to dawn upon so many Christians is the fact that we carry about within our bodies—our "earthen vessels"—treasures of inestimable value. If we could only realize the wealth of resources that we carry about, all the anxiety, fretting and worrying that we do would come to an abrupt end. In the person of the Lord of Glory, and in the person of the Holy

Spirit, there are resources abundant to meet every need that we could possibly ever have.

Realization of this great wealth and treasure would also cause other changes in our manners and attitudes. For instance, if you have only a dollar in your pocket, you can march gaily along the street and through the shops, knowing that if you should lose it, it matters little, for there is not much at stake. But if you have five thousand dollars in your pocket, there is a complete change of manners and attitude. While you will have great joy over having such a large sum, there will be no careless jaunting along the road —and every once in a while you will slacken your pace and reach and feel for your treasure and finding it still in place, you will smile and in joyful solemnity continue on.

How good it is for us to realize the wealth of the treasure that we have in our hearts. And, how good it is for us to slacken our pace in the busy routine of life, and feel for that treasure, and then, after being assured that it is still there, continue on in life.

Let us be reminded—and I say it with utmost reverence—we who have been born again, we carry *God* in our hearts! God, who brought the world, the universe into existence out of nothing, the miracle worker, the Ruler of the vast universe; God, greater and more powerful than we could ever understand, is the treasure tucked away in my heart—treasure in a vessel of clay.

As the manna from heaven was always more than enough, as the water abundantly flowed from the flinty rock, as the meal in the barrel was always enough, as the little boy's lunch grew into a banquet feast for over 5,000, as sure as God performed these miracles, we can be just as sure that our every need will be abundantly met in Him.

Put your smile back on—let its joy overflow your heart! Reach into your heart and feel again that treasure, and know in Him you have the answer. It is *Christ in you*—the hope of glory.

The Importance of Missions

> Go ye therefore, and teach all nations, baptizing them in the name of the Father, and of the Son, and of the Holy Ghost.
>
> MATTHEW 28:19

There are two reasons why a concerted missions program is vital to the life and blessings of a local church or individual. First, there is consideration and obedience to the command of Christ to *go* with the *Gospel*. No church or no person can live in direct disobedience to that command or any other command of Christ and have His blessings. When we give serious consideration to his Word and make a conscious effort to obey, then the blessings of God will rest upon us—I want to make absolutely clear that while this command takes into its scope the entire church, it was a command given to individuals for the promise of Jesus is: "I'll go with *you*"—thus He was addressing them as individuals. I say this because oft times people in the church speak of what their church is doing to carry out His command, WHILE DOING NOTHING THEMSELVES! Such individuals are like a desert in an oasis, everyone around them is living with the refreshing life sustaining presence of Jesus and there they sit, drying up, blessingless, selfish and self-centered—wondering!

The second reason that missions is vital to a church is this: It keeps us aware and conscious of the necessity of being soul winners—witnesses. Churches and individuals *die spiritually* because they become too occupied with *activities* unrelated to the salvation of lost men.

Missions keeps us on the right track, on center and target. It is impossible for anyone or any church to overemphasize missions! It just can't be done. As we think of this, think of another impossibility that looms before us. It is impossible to keep a church from growing and seeing souls saved that gives heavy emphasis to missions.

As I write this, the words of our Lord come to mind: "Seek ye first the Kingdom of God and His righteousness . . . and all these other things shall be added unto you!" The Kingdom comes *first*! But what is the Kingdom? It is SOULS! For the King is not the Kingdom, the subjects are. Now you can no more have the Kingdom without the King than you can have sunshine without the sun. But the Kingdom is made up of you and me, people of every nation and tribe that have received the Gospel. Seek the Kingdom *first*. We dare not relegate missions to a last place positions; missions must have first priority!

Catching Men

And he saith unto them, "Follow me, and I will make you fishers of men."

MATTHEW 4:19

Walk into any sporting goods store that in any way caters to fishermen, and you will find a myriad of lures displayed—all of which, according to their manufacturer, can't fail to catch fish.

But the reason there are more fish than there are people is not due to the lack of fishermen; it is due to the failure of fishermen to catch fish. Now, fishermen excuse their failure by such things as "they're not biting today." (The fish have gone on a hunger strike against fishermen!) Too much wind, too cold, too warm, too dry, too much rain, too still, too much noise.

But what about we fishers of men? After all, what Jesus really said was "follow me, and I will teach you to catch men." Our success as fishers of men, then, depends upon how close we follow our Teacher and how observant we are to His teachings and methods.

Observing Jesus through the Scriptures, we find that He always seemed to have just the right touch. Remember that, a little four-letter word comes to mind: TACT. Tact is a word that is derived from a French and Latin word, "to touch." it is the delicate perception of the right thing to do or say without causing offense. As we think about "catching men," allow me to break it down as follows:

T — Think. Yes, think, man! Is the action you are about to take really wise? Put yourself for a moment in the other person's shoes. Would you appreciate being treated thus? 'T' could also stand for Timing, for the right time is certainly essential to catching men. In thinking it over, will your move at this time cause the person to be offended? Yes, *think*, brother.

A — Action. No use to think unless you are going to act. You must cast out the bait ... Sow the seed ... Reach out to the *lost* ... Not all activity results in a catch! A flurry of activity doesn't always mean that souls are being saved. Because you have noise, doesn't mean you're having revival.

C — Commit. You're put the bait out, you've sown the seed. Now, you don't catch fish with the bait on the ground, and you don't harvest potatoes if you remove from the ground every ten days. Commit. You can't *make* fish bite, but we know that sooner or later, they will.

T — Trust. Trust God. You've sown the seed; you've thrown out the bait. Now, the seed is the *Word!* The Father says that it will spring forth, that it is good seed. I think of the bait as our personal experience and testimony. Our love for Christ which is not love for a denomination or movement, but a genuine love for Christ—so absolutely genuine that it removes all doubts as to whether we are sincere or not.

Yes, TACT or the right *touch* is of utmost importance. Without it, you will probably go home empty-handed.

The Twelve Gates Were
Twelve Pearls

> And the twelve gates were twelve pearls: every
> several gate was of one pearl: and the street of the
> city was pure gold, as it were transparent glass.
>
> REVELATION 21:21

It is interesting to note that the gates to the New
Jerusalem are not diamonds, rubies, or other
precious stones, but *pearls*.

Pearls, unlike any other jewel, are drawn
from the animate creation. Pearls are produced
by life. A life that has reacted to and overcome
the working of death. It is *only* when the oyster is
wounded that it produces its pearl. Isaiah says,
"He [Jesus] was wounded for our trans-
gressions" (53:5). Had it not been for this
wounding of our Lord, there would be no
"Gates of Pearl"—no access whatever for you
and me. As the oyster builds a pearl around that
foreign object that has wounded it, so Jesus took
our iniquities; and, bearing them, though foreign
to Him, became sin for us and covered that sin
with His precious life's blood, thereby creating a
gateway of pearl for you and me to enter
through to eternal life.

Now as the oyster creates the pearl from a
wound—in yielding up the pearl, it must give up

its life. The pearl only comes into our lives through death. Up to this time, the pearl is hid in the life of the oyster.

What a parallel this is with Christ. Old Testament saints knew of a city, but nothing about the entrance into it. But through the wounding and death of Jesus, the Way, entrance was made plain. These gates of *pearl* came from His riven side. John said "the twelve gates were twelve pearls." Now while there are *twelve* gates, *there are not twelve ways.* For "every several gate was of one pearl" Jesus said, "I am the Way, the Truth, and the Life" (John 14:6). He is the pearl of great price. He is the gate of pearl which we shall pass through to life everlasting.

Myths!

Myths! A myth is a fable, tale, talk; a story, the origin of which is forgotten, especially associated with some religious belief. ... A thing existing only in the imagination.

Let's look at some old religious myths of which I am sure I know the origin. I am convinced that a lot of things that people hold to as truth today have their origin in the pit of hell, for they are certainly not biblical.

First of all, let's look at that ridiculous idea or myth continually perpetuated by many that all you have to do to get to heaven is just "be good." This old tale springs up like dandelions and is just as hardy, but it does not have one smell of the truth about it. How utterly ridiculous to think that Almighty God would waste His Son on Calvary if all that man had to do to be saved was just to "be good." Now, being good is certainly a virtue not to be ignored, but it is not our goodness that saves us, but *His* goodness, *His* righteousness.

It is sad indeed to know that thousands of men and women are led to believe this fable—or, more appropriately, a lie. For it is taught from many a pulpit by a weak-kneed, watered-down version of what a preacher is supposed to be and teach. Jesus did not waste time to talk about the weather, politics, religion, or war to Nicodemus; Jesus didn't take the time to comment on his robe or question where he had his sandals made, but head-on, without hesitation, Jesus told Nicodemus he *must be born again!*

There is no other way but Jesus, for it was Jesus who said, "I am *the* Way." Not *a* way, but *the* Way. Not *another* way, but *the* Way. Not better than *other* ways, but *the* Way, *the* Truth, *the* Life.

Your goodness may enable men to walk past your casket and say, "we'll miss him, for he was a *good* man." But it will never enable God to say the words we long to hear most—"enter in thou *good and faithful servant*, to the joys of eternal life."

Another Myth Exploded

Some teach repentance and confession of sin are no longer necessary—ALL that men must do is believe and accept Christ.

Let's look at the facts of God's Word. First of all, the Bible does teach that "whosoever calls upon the name of the Lord shall be saved," and also if you believe in your heart and confess with your mouth the Lord Jesus, that God raised Him from the dead, "thou shalt be saved" (Rom. 10:13,9). But these Scriptures *must* be understood and taken with the rest of the Bible's teaching on salvation and not separate or apart from it.

The fact is, that repentance is taught *more* in the New Testament than the Old, and *more* since the cross in the New Testament than *before* the cross—in not one passage do we find that men *are not* to repent, pray, confess, or seek God since the cross.

The fact is, before the cross, Christ and others commanded all men to "repent and believe the gospel" (Mark 1:15, 6:12) and "except ye repent, ye shall all likewise perish" (Luke

13:3-5). Christ repeatedly said that he came to call "sinners to repentance" (Matt. 9:13) and there was "rejoicing in heaven over one sinner that repented" (Luke 15:1-7).

Since the cross, Christ commanded the disciples "that *repentance* and remission of sins should be preached in His name *among all nations.*" At Pentecost, Peter, obeying the command of Jesus, commanded them to "repent and be baptised *every one of you.*" Peter wrote in his second epistle that "the Lord is not willing that any should perish but that all should come to repentance." Jesus commanded men to repent as late as 96 A.D. when the last book of the Bible was written. (See Rev. 2:5, 11, 18, 21; 3:3, 19.)

The fact is, if men want to be saved, they must *repent* of and turn from their sins and walk and live according to the pattern that Jesus set before us, for "he that saith he abideth in Him ought himself also to walk, even as He (Jesus) walked."

Some Things Are Impossible

And beside this, giving all diligence, add to your faith virtue; and to virtue knowledge; and to knowledge temperance; and to temperance patience; and to patience godliness; and to godliness brotherly kindness; and to brotherly kindness charity. For if these things be in you, and abound, they make you that ye shall neither be barren nor unfruitful in the knowledge of our Lord Jesus Christ. But he that lacketh these things is blind, and cannot see afar off, and hath forgotten that he was purged from his old sins.

2 PETER 1:5-9

It is impossible for you to fly by flapping your arms as an eagle flaps his wings. It is impossible to live long without a drink of water. It is impossible to survive without food, and it is *impossible to be a fruitful Christian* if you lack the spiritual grace Peter writes about in these verses. If you lack, Peter says you are blind and cannot see, but if they be in you and about ... they make sure that ye shall neither be *barren* nor *unfruitful* in the knowledge of our Lord Jesus Christ.

We need to remember the words of Jesus wherein He said, "Follow me, and *I will make you fishers of men.*" It is impossible to be a fisher of men without being a devoted, dedicated, Spirit-led follower of Jesus Christ. Now, I have written in somewhat a negative view, just to capture your thinking. So let me turn your thoughts from the impossible to the possible. Add these virtues and graces to your life so that you may be fruitful. Seek God for His presence in your life. Walk, live, sing, pray in the Spirit, abandon carnal thinking, and follow Jesus.

The New Birth

> Whosoever believeth that Jesus is the Christ is born of God: and every one that loveth him that begat loveth him also that is begotten of him.
>
> 1 JOHN 5:1

Every "born again" child of God has the threefold proof of the new birth—proof that *he* is a *child of God*.

There is, first of all, the "inward proof" spoken of in 1 John 5:1: "Whosoever believeth that Jesus is the Christ is born of God." Believing must be more than just a lip service! Romans 10:9 teaches that we must believe in our hearts. *Some people are only 16 inches from heaven,* for that is the distance from an average man's head to his heart. Many people say with the mind, "I believe," but never believe in their heart; but it is "with the *heart*, man believeth," and it doesn't stop with mere believing—it is a believing unto *righteousness* or right doing.

Believing unto righteousness or right doing brings us to the second proof or the "outward proof" of the new birth. 1 John 2:29 says, "Everyone that doeth righteousness is born of Him." If you are born again—born of God—*you will do righteously*, at all times, at all costs. This is outward proof of an inward work. The "born again" child of God doesn't have to be bound by contract, for he will live by his word; nor does he have to be kept under constant surveillance, for he will not steal, and we could go on and on. ... Remember this! The child of God will seek ways to practice righteousness at all times.

The third proof is "outgoing proof": "Everyone that loveth is born of God." (See 1 John 4:7-11.) We are to love our fellowman to the extent that we love as God loved us. God loved us when we rejected and despised Him. We must let God love man through us in like manner. We are to love our enemies and pray for those that despitefully use us. By nature, we can't do this, but when we are the "born again" child of God, we can! This love for all men is the "outgoing proof" that we have become a "new creature in Christ."

Was Cain an Atheist?

Woe unto them! for they have gone in the way of Cain, and ran greedily after the error of Balaam for reward, and perished in the gainsaying of Core [Korah].

JUDE 11

An atheist is one who *denies* the existence of God. The English word *atheist* is taken from the Greek word, *atheos. A-* meaning 'not'; plus *theos*, meaning 'God.' Hence the meaning, *no God!*

Cain was not an atheist, but he was perhaps, the *first modernist!* Modernism believes in religion, but not salvation. Modernism believes *in* God, but does not *believe* God. This is a picture of the world today. Openly proclaiming they believe *in* God, but day by day ignoring the plain truth of the Scriptures. Modernism celebrates what is said to be His birthday, and commemorates His resurrection, but calmly rejects the purpose for which He came.

Modernism substitutes religion for righteousness; ethics for Bible essentials; service for salvation; and culture for confession. These things are like putting a bandaid on a cancer! They fall hopelessly short of what is needed for the cure of mankind's illness.

Cain brought a beautiful offering, satisfying to the eyes of man, but not to the eyes of God.

Cain's offering was the result of his labor, toil and sweat. Abel's offering was the first of the flock, the gift of God, for he had done nothing but simply bring it and offer it to God. It was bloody, gory, bleeding, repulsive and unappealing, *but* it was what God had required.

Modernism ignores the requirement of repentance, confession and faith. Modernism is the way of compromise and tolerance, rejecting the necessity of being washed in the blood of the Lamb and substituting mere religion which came into existence before Cain, making the cross of Christ of none effect.

No, Cain wasn't an atheist. He is just like some of you who will read this. Some of you will continue in your own way, believing *in* God, but refusing to *believe Him* and *obey* His Word.

What Is the Baptism with Fire?

John answered, saying unto them all, "I indeed baptize you with water; but one mightier than I cometh, the latchet of whose shoes I am not worthy to unloose: he shall baptize you with the Holy Ghost and with fire."

LUKE 3:16

What is the baptism with fire?

We know without question what the baptism with the Holy Ghost is. It is a coming of the Holy Spirit into a life in all His fullness. It is receiving the Spirit without measure. It is being immersed in the mighty floodtide of the Holy Spirit's power until the flesh is energized and quickened and the lips burst forth with praise in a language foreign to us but known unto God. It is joy unspeakable and full of glory.

What about the baptism with fire? Are we to pray for fire? If I understand the Scripture, the fire accompanies the Spirit baptism whether we pray for it or not. Is this fire, zeal, enthusiasm, exuberance? Is it the fire that causes people to shout and rejoice with loud praises? Is that the fire John was speaking about?

Notice now that John speaks of fire again in the next verse—unquenchable fire burning up the chaff. The wheat He gathers into His garner. What is the chaff? Sinners? Ungodly men? No!

The chaff is that undesirable husk; that thing that is of no value and that was once fastened to the wheat. Certainly the wheat represents the Christian, and if that is so, then the chaff is that undesirable, valueless thing in their life that was once a part of them, that is shaken off by the activity of the threshing floor and burned in the fire.

Did not the apostles and believers in the early church experience the fire—persecution, torture, martyrdom! Oh, yes, they had the fire, didn't they?

No, you don't need to pray for the fire. You just yield completely to Christ, and certainly the fire will come. Sure, the flesh will kick and fuss about surrendering the chaff up to the fire. But the precious Holy Spirit will continually abide to refresh you again and again.

Perfecting Holiness in the Life

Be ye not unequally yoked together with unbelievers: for what fellowship hath righteousness with unrighteousness? and what communion hath light with darkness? And what concord hath Christ with Belial? or what part hath he that believeth with an infidel? And what agreement hath the temple of God with idols? for ye are the temple of the living God; as God hath said, I will dwell in them, and walk in them; and I will be their God, and they shall be my people.

Wherefore come out from among them, and be ye separate, saith the Lord, and touch not the unclean thing; and I will receive you. And will be a Father unto you, and ye shall be my sons and daughters, saith the Lord Almighty.

2 CORINTHIANS 6:14-18

Every child of God must have holiness as their ultimate goal in this life. For those who many have missed last week's article, allow me to define again the term *holiness*. Holiness is the absolute surrender to the will (Word) of God in all things great and small.

Now, while surrender speaks of the first step in achieving holiness in any degree, it is certainly not all. To surrender involves one act: simply the giving up of ourselves unto God. The attitude we take about our surrender is important, too. During World War II, there were men captured by the U.S. forces that considered such as a rescue; they were delighted to be taken prisoners. There were others who, though they surrendered, they were always defiant and rebellious. Perhaps this is not a good comparison to draw, but the Scriptures place a lot of emphasis on the need of the whole man to be completely surrendered to God.

To perfect holiness in the life, some other things must be required. When we surrender, we put ourselves at His mercy, but we can't stay in that passive state. So another word, "separation," comes into focus. One of the meanings of the word "separate" is to "go in different directions." So when we are born again, the prison doors are opened; the fetters are broken; we are friends with God; now we are holy, for the blood has cleansed us from all sin. But now, we must separate ourselves; we must go in a different direction. We must separate ourselves from unequal yokes with unbelievers. There is danger involved with fellowship with the unsaved. To visit to win people to God is one thing. To fellowship with the unrighteous, going to banquets and feasts, is another; and certainly no sane Christian single person should ever even date an unsaved person.

Notice that Paul writes of separation from unrighteousness; separation from darkness; a separation [change] of affection from idols to

Christ; a separation from the unclean (or foul) thing—unclean thoughts, speech, attitudes, etc. Then and only then do we have the promise "I will receive you and will be a Father unto you."

Now, if you doubt the importance I have placed upon separation, look at what the Scriptures say about Lot. Contrast him with Abraham who lived a separated life. The Scriptures say that Lot vexed his righteous soul by the deeds of those around him. He didn't have to live in Sodom, but he did.

You are subject to the atmosphere you live in. No wise Christian who values his relationship with God will permit himself to be found in any place that will subject his soul to annoyances created by the world. Friendship with the world is enmity with God (James 4:4). One thing is for certain: when you can't tell the church and the world one from another, rest assured, it isn't the world that has changed.

Perfecting Holiness in the Life through Service

> The disciple is not above his master, nor the servant above his lord. It is enough for the disciple that he be as his master, and the servant as his lord. If they have called the master of the house Beelzebub, how much more shall they call them of his household?
>
> MATTHEW 10:24-25

I have written about holiness through surrender and through separation. Surrender leaves us in a passive, neutral position, and separation speaks of positive, definite action in a negative sense, for it is separation from the world, evil associations, darkness and dishonesty. So now we come to the positive side of holiness. One can be surrendered, and live separated, but he is not perfect in holiness unless he knows the meaning of *service*.

One has said that service is the greatest word in our language. One thing is certain: none of us can be like our Lord unless we serve others.

In the text that I have given, Jesus said, "It is enough for the disciple that he be as his master." The ultimate goal then of discipleship is to be like Christ. To be like Him is to be holy, for who can deny His holiness? His life was an endless manifestation of service to others. He thought of Himself as a servant; we must think and act the same.

Service in the Biblical sense is an act of kindness done because of our devotion to another. We serve others because of our devotion to Christ. He served us because of His devotion to the Father. I do not paster because I am just devoted to my church or to my religion or to my denomination. If my devotion doesn't go higher than that, then I have not a smidgen above the man who works in a factory and is a devoted employee.

My work and service, if it is to be pleasing unto my Lord, must be the result of my ardent devotion to Him. Paul writes to the Philippians of those who preach Christ of envy and strife, of contention, not sincerely. So it is possible for what should be our service to be nothing more to us than a job—a piece of work. The difference being this: when it is done through devotion to Christ, we look forward to doing it. When it is merely a job, we look forward to being done with it. In service, we anticipate the task. In work, we anticipate the finish.

So then, true holiness involves service unto Christ, and the only way we can serve Him is in love, serving one another (Galatians 5:13).

Quit thinking of Bible holiness as a "taste not, touch not, handle not" experience only. Rather, think of it in the light of surrender, separation and service.

In conclusion, let me say that—

One cannot have Bible holiness and not be missions-minded. *Matt. 28:19-20.*

One cannot be holy and not love the Scriptures, for we are to study to show ourselves approved. *2 Tim. 2:15.*

One cannot be holy unless he is willing to forgive, because he will not be forgiven by the Father. *Matt. 6:15.*

One has not experienced Bible holiness unless he has humbled himself and is walking in obedience to the light he has received. For this was the mind of Christ: to be a servant, humble and obedient. *Phil. 2:5-8.*

It is enough of a disciple to be like his master. It is not too much. It is enough.

Follow Peace & Holiness

Follow peace with all men, and holiness, without which no man shall see the Lord:

HEBREWS 12:14

Today we deal with two things that are an absolute necessity if we hope to see God. These are not options that we can take or leave at our discretion; these are absolutes.

First, the Scripture says, "Follow peace." A better meaning would be, "*Pursue* peace." This puts the initiative upon us. Some are willing to be at peace with others if they do the pursuing, but they are not about to take action to bring about peace. Then we are to "pursue" or "seek" peace with *all* men. Not just a select few; not just those whose friendship or fellowship we don't want to lose, but *all* men.

Secondly, we come to this absolute requirement of holiness. Holiness has been confused by so many things conjured up in the minds of men until many are at a complete loss as to what it really is.

Let me begin by saying that holiness is not a *negative* thing. Holiness is not found in simply refraining from or abstaining from. Holiness is a positive experience in the heart of man. I like to define holiness as the *complete and absolute surrender to the will* (Word) *of God* in all things great and small. Holiness covers the entire sphere of our lives. It covers attitudes, desires, personal habits, worship, work, play, devotion, dress, prayer, etc. Holiness is simply allowing Him, our Lord, to govern and control our lives. It is living under His control. It is control by the Holy Spirit. Galatians 5:16 says, "Walk in the Spirit and ye shall not fulfill the lusts of the flesh." It is control by the Word. Psalm 119:11 says, "Thy word have I hid in mine heart, that I might not sin against thee." It is control by the Father. James 4:17 says, "Submit yourselves therefore to God. Resist the devil."

How often do people do just the opposite of what James says. They resist God and submit to the devil. Don't be the devil's stooge! Obey the Word and follow on to know the Lord.

Imitations!

Be ye followers of me, even as I also am of Christ.

1 CORINTHIANS 11:1

The world doesn't like imitations. What young lady wants an imitation diamond for her engagement? What woman wants a necklace of imitation pearls? And who wouldn't really rather have an original Rembrandt than an imitation?

An imitation, you see, is a copy. A copy of something *superior* or *genuine*. The apostle Paul in the above-mentioned text says, "Be ye followers [Greek, *mimetai*, imitators] of me, even as I also am of Christ." Paul is saying, "I am not the superior one; I'm just an imitation. An imitation is the result or product of imitating! The more I work at imitating Christ, the better imitation I become."

45

We all know there are various degrees of imitations. There is the cheap imitation which even the untrained eye can detect the flaws in dime-store merchandise that is easily and readily discernible. God help us to work at imitating Christ until the world has more respect for us as Christians than to look upon us as dime-store copy. Then there is the imitation that is so perfect that the experts argue about which is the original and which is the copy. Only the *creators* of the work know the difference. It was Paul that men thought was a god when, on the island of Melita, he shook the viper off into the fire with no ill effects. Paul was a great imitation of Christ, but while men wondered, the Creator knew the difference.

We can say with absolute authority that the world hates imitators of Christ, for He said the world would.

Now, when it comes to being an imitation of Christ, the opposite is true as concerning other things. For instance, when it comes to a work of art, the better the copy, the more it is appreciated; but when it comes to imitating Christ, the cheaper the copy, the more unlike the original, the more the world appreciates it. Ah, let the world think what it will; the chief occupation of every born again person is to work at imitating Christ until when men notice us they will look beyond the copy and see Jesus.

God Is!

God is a Spirit: and they that worship him must
worship him in spirit and in truth.

JOHN 4:24

John 4:24 says, "God is a spirit." First John 4:8
and 16 says God is love. The Scriptures tell us
God is light, and in Him is no darkness; that our
God is a consuming fire; and the psalmist
declared that God is a very present help in
trouble. These and other passages give us insight
into the nature and attributes of God. But for
those who may not be able to remember all of
these things about God, don't worry, for all you
really need to remember is simply this: God is.

God is our help, our hope, our health, our
happiness, our habitation.

God is our Judge, our joy, our jubilation and
our justification.

God is the giver of our peace, the source of
our power, the object of our praise and the
pattern of our lives.

God is liberty to the one in bondage, He is
light to the one in darkness, He is life to the one
in death and He is love to the one filled with
hate.

God is our compass over stormy seas of life,
He is our constant companion through life, He is

our courage when fear arises and He is our compensation when life is finished.

God is the source of our existence, the cause of our excitement, the means of our escape (from fears, frustration and hell), and the glory of our existence. He is also our expectation.

God is! God is our everything! Therefore there is no need for the child of God to shop the paltry marketplaces of this world, filled with the stench of sin and marked with the presence of death, for God is . . . our everything!

"Beloved, now are we the sons of God, and it doth not yet appear what we shall be: but we know that, when he shall appear, we shall be like him; for we shall see him as he is." (1 John 3:2)

What Is Wealth?

But godliness with contentment is great gain. For we brought nothing into this world, and it is certain we can carry nothing out. And having food and raiment let us be therewith content. But they that will be rich fall into temptation and a snare, and into many foolish and hurtful lusts, which drown men in destruction and perdition.

For the love of money is the root of all evil: which while some coveted after, they have erred from the faith, and pierced themselves through with many sorrows. But thou, O man of God, flee these things; and follow after righteousness, godliness, faith, love, patience, meekness.

1 TIMOTHY 6:6-11

Who is a wealthy man? Can you say that the world's richest men are the world's wealthiest? Godliness with contentment is great gain (or wealth), Paul writes, and if we have food and raiment, let us be therewith content. In other words, if we have sufficient material goods and godliness, we should have contentment, which is one of the most sought after things in this life.

True wealth cannot be measured by the amount one possesses. It was our Lord who said that a man's life consisteth not in the abundance of things which he possesses. Certainly there were men with great possessions in the Scripture: Job, Abraham, Isaac, Jacob, for example. But these were men who rules their riches instead of allowing their riches to rule them. This is the key! Abraham left his homeland to follow God to the promised land. Certainly he surrendered title to much he owned, to obey God. Job lost everything but his faith! He refused to curse God at the suggestion of his wife.

Most everyone in this nation has sufficient material goods, and many have an abundance. Many of you who read this also live godly lives, but still many of you have not found that blessed state of contentment. *Beware of covetousness!* It is one of the most deadly of evils. It robs one of the sweet contentment he finds in Jesus. Many have fallen into this snare and have pierced themselves through with many sorrows. We can't really visualize money (or the love of it, covetousness) doing that to us, can we? We visualize money as producing happiness. It can, but it depends entirely on you. God must be first in your finances. The tithe is to be paid or given first, not last. This is the divine order: Jesus—Others—Yourself. It is not just accidental that the first letters of each word spell JOY. It is rather providential. Divine providence desires that when our lives assume this order, then we have joy and contentment.

The Scripture warns us to flee coveting after riches and follow after righteousness. Godliness, faith, love, patience, meekness—all qualities that further ensure us of a wealth of joy and contentment in this life and in the life to come.

You are going to leave this world with empty hands, regardless of how much or how little they have held in life. This is self-evident. However, we do not have to live here or leave here with empty hearts. We can live and leave in the sweet contentment of the God-filled life.

It is said of Stephen that he was full of the Holy Ghost, full of wisdom, full of faith and power, and he was filled with a vision in death, crying, "I see Jesus"; and he was full of mercy and compassion, for he said: "Lay not this sin to their account. Poor Stephen? No! Never! He died on his knees and without malice to this murderers. He had nothing in his hands, but oh, what he had in his heart! God filled his being, and God received him to eternal habitations.

Weapons and Warfare

(For the weapons of our warfare are not carnal, but mighty through God to the pulling down of strong holds;) Casting down imaginations, and every high thing that exalteth itself against the knowledge of God, and bringing into captivity every thought to the obedience of Christ.

2 CORINTHIANS 10:4-5

This passage is openly suggestive to a fact we would so often like to forget; nevertheless, we cannot.

Paul, first of all, mentions our weaponry— not carnal, or natural, but mighty through God. Though we live in the flesh, we do not war after the flesh. The flesh likes to flex its muscles, show off its bulging biceps and lightning-fast reflexes. How well do we remember the strutting, goose-stepping, nattily-attired armies of Hitler in the

'40s; and what a show of military might does, the great powers of the world still display even today. So it is with the flesh, but not with the Spirit. The spiritual man never resorts to any of these things; no, never. He is not interested in trying to display his ability. The spiritual man has learned to humble himself; to afflict his soul by fasting and relying completely upon the power of Jesus Christ. No flexing the muscles, but a bending of the knees; no boasting, but a breaking of our wills, submitting ourselves to God.

The strength of our arsenal is not in our might, but His might. In fact, we do not have to have strength, because the victory is not in our strength but in the power of the Holy Spirit. I was made to realize this sometime ago when I was weak in body from fasting and trying to pray; everything was a great effort. God made me to know that the victory was mine, that His strength was sufficient and that much could be accomplished for Him through the use of the weapons of fasting and prayer, regardless of how feeble I am.

Secondly, Paul writing in the Spirit mentions our warfare. Certainly the mention of weapons alone would point to a warfare. Why would God put weapons at our disposal if there were no battle? The battle rages, the battle lines have been drawn for a long time. Satan also has literally millions of missionaries and ambassadors of evil. Look at the army he controls in the battle for the bodies and souls of men. Nearly every TV program is flooded with vulgarities or suggestive phrases. The radio programs play suggestive music, glorifying free sex, dope, an open society—Satan has legions of pensmen, spewing from the pen—blasphemies, profanity, and the most vulgar of expressions, making one wonder how a person conceives of such things. Satan has an army of soothsaying preachers, denying the blood of Jesus, advocating an open society where everyone is free to do as he or she pleases. Satan has his legions advocating the open and free use of drugs; men and women literally preaching the use of marijuana, LSD, STP, etc. He seeks control of mind, body and soul through these things.

I've painted a dismal pictures perhaps, yet I've not told all. Satan is mighty, but God is almighty. Satan has his millions; sure he has the majority in numbers, but numbers never did amount to much when God fights a battle through His people. "One shall chase a thousand, but two shall put ten thousand to flight." (Deut. 32:30)

We have the mightiest of weaponry; weapons mighty through God to the tearing down of the strongholds of Satan, bringing into captivity every though, casting down everything that exalteth itself against the knowledge of God. God help us to employ the weapons of submission, humility, prayer and fasting. We're in a battle, but remember, the word "defeat" does not belong in the Christian's vocabulary.

Glorify God in Your Body

> For ye are bought with a price: therefore glorify God in your body, and in your spirit, which are God's.

1 CORINTHIANS 6:20

Hundreds of tents made up the camp of Israel, but there was one tent in the midst of the camp that was quite different from the rest. Now, it didn't look too different as far as outward appearance. It looked fairly well like the rest except perhaps for the size of it. You could do as you pleased in the other tents, eat or fast, work or relax, sing, talk or meditate. But this one tent commanded reverence and awe. When men approached, they did so reverently and quietly. Children played games in and around other tents, but not this one. One thing made this tent different: the Shekinah glory of the living God, signifying God's presence. This tent was made by direction from God and for the express purpose of providing a place for God to dwell among His people.

You are the temple of the Holy Ghost; so declares the apostle Paul in the New Testament. How we need to understand, that when we were born again, our bodies became the dwelling place of God. Certainly we are different! Different, not because of being made of different material—we are still mortal, still human flesh. Just as all the tents were made by human hands and of the same materials, so there is no difference in this sense between us and other men.

As in the Old Testament tabernacle, so in the New Testament temple—the difference is God! The divine glow of His presence sets us apart. Old Testament saints did not go to the tabernacle to worship a tent. They went to worship God. God's design was on the tent, and everything pointed to the worship of the Holy One of Israel. The same will be true of you and me if we allow God to work out His design, His plan, His will in our lives. Our life will glorify (exalt, praise, lift up, point to) God. And isn't this totally in accord with New Testament truth? "Ye are living epistles"—letter messages—"known and read of all men." Let us so live and worship so that we may be sure the world will get the right message.

Cross Control

"Now is my soul troubled; and what shall I say? Father, save me from this hour: but for this cause came I unto this hour. Father, glorify thy name." Then came there a voice from heaven, saying, "I have both glorified it, and will glorify it again."

JOHN 12:27-28

The Gospel of John gives us insight in the feelings of Jesus Christ as no other Gospel does. In the above mentioned passage, we have revealing the inner feelings and anxieties of Christ. His soul is "troubled." Troubled about what? Troubled about facing the agonies of the cross—troubled about the battle that would take place on Calvary—a battle in which He would openly triumph over the devil, spoiling him and putting him to public shame. But this would be no easy victory. This victory would bring Him into that awful experience of being abandoned —forsaken—by the Father. An experience He had never known before. An experience so horrible, that each moment of it must seem like an eternity. Yet in view of all this, He was ruled by the cross.

These words fell from His lips: "For this cause came I unto this hour." These are not the words of a fatalist, who says "what is to be will be." But these are the words of one on a mission, one under control, one whose every step and action is decisive and takes Him one step closer to His goal—Jesus was controlled by the cross? How we need in our lives this experience—this submission to the Rule of the Cross.

Paul, that beloved apostle to the Gentiles, experienced this Cross Control. His pen shouts these words in Galatians 6:14: "God forbid that I should glory save [except] in the cross of our Lord Jesus Christ, by whom the world is crucified unto me, and I unto the world."

The songwriter penned it thus: "A lonely cross became His throne." So there is such a thing as Rule *from* the Cross in the songwriter's mind—but I think it more expedient to be *ruled by the cross*—"controlled by the cross"—or, more simply, by what the cross represents: submission, sacrifice, reproach, *the death of self.*

Jesus lived, and His purpose in living was to die on the cross. His earthly life began in a manger and ended at Calvary. Our life begins at Calvary and will end in Glory, not in death but in abundant life.

We need to impale "self" on the cross and from this experience, let that "new man" emerge which after God is created in righteousness and true holiness. (See Eph. 4:24.)

In the natural, we have a feeling for the place we were born, and we come under the rule of the nation we were born in; I think the same is true of those "born again." It happened at the cross ... Oh, how I love to visit Calvary again and again … And oh! How I love that wonderful feeling when I've said "yes" to the Rule of the Cross!

I Have Been Crucified with Christ!

> I am crucified with Christ: nevertheless I live; yet not I, but Christ liveth in me: and the life which I now live in the flesh I live by the faith of the son of God, who loved me, and gave himself for me.

GALATIANS 2:20

Crucified! What does this mean? I haven't been nailed to a cross. I haven't been beaten with stripes; neither was Paul, at the start of his ministry, but he writes of being Crucified with Christ.

First of all, it simply means to die with Christ. Now an important thing to remember about death is the finality of it, life is ended; death has captured and taken life prisoner with no reprieve. Paul writes, "I am crucified (dead), yet I live, Yet Not I, Christ liveth in me." Here seems to be the key. Paul is saying with finality: I'm dead, yet I live; but it's not really Paul any longer for he is dead but it is Christ. I'm dead, and buried with me in that death is all my dreams, aspirations, and plans for my life. Now it is Christ living in me, and the life I live in the flesh, I even live that life by the faith of Jesus; it's not even my faith that I'm living by, but His. He loved me, Paul writes, and gave Himself for me. I am living because of the triumph of His faith at Calvary. I am dead; I have no right to any claim of personal achievement. I don't even live anymore; I'm crucified and Christ lives within me.

That, my good friend, is the meaning of Crucifixion. Jesus could have called ten thousand angels, but He did not. What He did do, was throw away the rights that we lay claim to so often. As the song writer put it, "He kept on walking up the Hill, He knew what He was doing but He kept on still." Yes, Jesus died for the Love of Me!

Careful for Nothing

> Be careful for nothing; but in every thing by prayer and supplication with thanksgiving let your requests be made known unto God.
>
> PHILIPPIANS 4:6

Be careful for nothing; don't worry about *anything*. This is Paul's word of encouragement to the Philippian Christians who had given out of their own need to provide for the Jerusalem saints.

The psalmist said in Psalm 5:11: "Let all those that put their trust in Thee rejoice, because Thou defendest them." God help us to trust You without terms, unconditionally.

The average Christian today has two major problems with himself. Number One is worry; worry *is not* faith; it is not trust; rather, to worry is to doubt. Number Two is spelling out the conditions upon which we want God to answer prayer for us. But God doesn't answer us according to the terms we spell out, but according to his wisdom, which is far above ours.

Let us pray as the disciple did, "Lord, help our unbelief," for without faith, it is impossible to please God.

The Root of Bitterness

... lest any root of bitterness springing up trouble you, and thereby many be defiled.

HEBREWS 12:15

Bitterness in one's life is here described as a root, springing up. Roots lie harmless in the soil through the winter months, showing no evidence of life whatsoever until the warm days of spring.

There is among us all and in us all the possibility of bitterness, malice, hate, etc. The harm does not come from the root of such things being in one's life. The harm comes when we allow conditions in our life to be altered and get so out of touch with Christ that the climate of our life allows these things to spring up or come to life. This passage teaches us to continue looking diligently for the coming of our Lord, lest any man fail of the grace of God. Now, we know that the grace of God is not going to fail, so this root of bitterness does not spring up because of failure on God's part. Bitterness comes to life because of our failure to diligently look for (i.e. keep before us) the Lord's coming.

When we look away from His coming, what do we see? We see the world; we become awake of our appetites for worldly pleasures and the desire to satisfy the flesh. We become like Esau who lost sight of the blessing when his stomach began to growl with hunger pains. When we look away from His coming, we provide the climate for bitterness to spring into life, for we begin to feel like life is passing us by, and we've given our time and money to God and what have we got to show for it? Such conditions of the life allow bitterness toward the church, the Christian, the preacher and even God to fill one's being. It troubles you, and if allowed to continue, will cause the defilement of others— possibly your children, your loved ones, friends. It troubles you, for bitterness hurts no one as much as the person who harbors it.

Christ is our hope, our only hope. If we look at life as the natural man, it is foolish to go to church, to give to the church, to sacrifice one's own desires. But when we realize that in this life, Christ is our only hope and that He gives us purpose in life, then we look not for rewards and pleasures here, but we look for Him who shall give us eternal reward. Such diligently looking for Jesus eliminates the possibility of a climate existing where bitterness can spring into life.

Keep looking: lest!

Who Did Sin?

And his disciples asked him, saying, "Master, who did sin, this man, or his parents, that he was born blind?"

JOHN 9:2

The disciples raised this question as Jesus was about to heal a man born blind, for some of the Jews believed souls came back into bodies as a penalty for sins in a previous life. Controversy often raged over whether some physical infirmity was the result of one's sins before birth, even in the womb, or sins by the parents.

Jesus answered that none of this was the cause of this man's blindness, and regardless of the cause, God's power will be manifest in his healing.

Jesus resolved this question of responsibility, but what about others?

Visualize if you can, a young man sitting in a cell awaiting the hour of his scheduled execution. He was judged by a jury and found guilty of assaulting a young lady. No question of his guilt? No!

But let's look a little farther. Could it be that this young man sits in death row because of a generation of lax, lukewarm, pampering, whimpering, compromising clergy that has torn God's Book apart and mocked at His demands of holiness in our living—men who have failed to warn others of the terrible consequences of departing from God's Word? Do they not share in the young man's guilt?

Could it be that this young man is guilty of attacking a girl who has an anxious mother that encouraged her daughter to dramatize and display her body in a fashion to attract young men to her, and something snapped in this youth until he was no longer able to remain rational? Does not the girl and her mother share in the guilt?

Think about it! Sin and guilt have far-reaching effects, but the cure is in Jesus. Help us to so live, Lord, that our actions and deeds are pleasing to you.

The Word That Pierces Brings Peace

> For the word of God is quick, and powerful, and sharper than any two-edged sword, piercing even to the dividing asunder of soul and spirit, and of the joints and marrow, and is a discerner of the thoughts and intents of the heart.
>
> HEBREWS 4:12

Some men lay great emphasis on rightly dividing the Word of truth, and it is true that the Scripture tells us we are to do this (2 Tim. 2:15); but it also tells us His Word is to divide us. Too often there is an attempt to divide the Word first, before we have allowed it to do its work on us.

The Word is not written for or to the intellect, but for the heart of man. It is not a book that we can study and analyze as any other book. We may find it strange that the Holy Spirit did not give us through the writers of the Word, a detailed handbook of Christian doctrines. How easily God could have done this and settled all theological debate. . . . But He did not!

The Word is a discerner of the thoughts and intents of the heart. Again, we remind you this is a book for the heart. Preachers are praised when they feed the intellect. They have been imprisoned and executed for preaching the Word in such a way that it cut to the heart. John the Baptist was; Stephen was. It wasn't theological treats and intellectual tidbits that they delivered. It was the truth—plain, clear, unmistakable—plunging like a dagger to the heart, calling for separation and division from sin.

These were men who had had that same powerful Word cut the heart of sin out of them. They had experienced first-hand the pain of the piercing Word, cutting away until the heart was bare before God. But while the Word first of all brings pain, it also brings peace, but only after we have allowed it to divide us from the affections and lust we held for the world.

Too many people are searching the Word for a loophole through which they can justify their sin, and wondering all the time why they can't find peace. Two things are glaringly plain in the Word: there is no justification for sin, and there is no peace without complete surrender to the will—and Word—of God.

Let the Word live, cut, divide and separate from you those things which would hinder your peace and eternal hope.

At Thy Word

"Nevertheless at thy word I will let down the net."

LUKE 5:5

Luke's Gospel gives us insight into the call of Peter, Andrew, James and John that Matthew's Gospel omits. In Matthew, we have the facts of the matter; in Luke, we have all the details. Matthew mentions nothing about the press of people wanting to hear the Word of God. Luke tells us it was this occasion that Jesus reveals Himself as Lord over creation. He had already revealed Himself as Lord over demon spirits. Jesus had already visited Simon's house and had healed Simon's mother-in-law. John's Gospel tells us Andrew introduced Peter to Jesus.

It is significant to note that while Peter knew Jesus and called Him "Master," it was only after the miraculous catch of fish that Peter confessed his sin and called Jesus "Lord." Peter had registered his despair in his words to Jesus: "We have toiled all night and caught nothing; nevertheless at thy word, I will let down the net." This was not an act of faith—it was an act of obedience. I think Peter expected another empty haul. He certainly did not anticipate what happened.

It is frequent in life that we exhaust the energies of the flesh in an attempt to do something for God. Too often, we find ourselves aching, tired and sore, carrying out some responsibility simply through obedience. And like Peter, we are just as amazed at the results.

It is important to note, too, that they had given up, quit. They had brought the ships in and James and John were washing and mending their nets. Peter was persuaded to get back in his ship so Jesus could use it as a pulpit to preach to the people from. Many times it is after we have quit striving in the flesh that we experience the blessings of God.

We do many things because of training, influence of others, or the desire to do what others do. *Doing* is not the mistake. *Doing without a word from our Lord* is where the fault lies.

Three things lie at the feet of the Christian. One: the possibility of doing nothing. Two: the possibility of doing in the energy of the flesh, possibly resulting in empty nets. Three: the possibility of doing, acting and doing by the Word of God, with blessings and results.

While one may be criticized sometimes for doing things in the energy of the flesh, it is good to remember that Peter was able to let down the net at the Word of Jesus because he had been doing. Those who never do anything would not be able to do, if Jesus spoke to them. Jesus never called one sitting idle to do His work. It was Phillip that called Nathaniel from sitting under the fig tree, not Jesus.

Are There "Extraordinary Men of God"?

> ... The effectual fervent prayer of a righteous man availeth much. Elias was a man subject to like passions as we are, and he prayed earnestly that it might not rain: and it rained not on the earth by the space of three years and six months.
>
> JAMES 5:16-17

> And I fell at his feet to worship him. And he said unto me, "See thou do it not: I am thy fellowservant, and of thy brethren that have the testimony of Jesus: worship God: for the testimony of Jesus is the spirit of prophecy."
>
> REVELATION 19:10

One of the problems facing Christians today is the temptation to give blind devotion to their leaders. Such a devotion is completely contrary to the Scriptures.

Now, if there ever was a preacher that could lay claim to the title "extraordinary man of God," it could have been Moses or Elijah. Strange as it may sound though, Moses had difficulty even getting the respect he deserved. And Elijah, as the Scripture teaches us in James, was just an ordinary man, subject to passions as we are, with one distinction: he was a man of prayer.

A lot of Christians today are falling victim to leaders who promote themselves as "great men of God." One may think that they are men who pray, but they are really men that "prey." While pretending to be men with a burden for souls, they are men with a greater burden for personal gain. While they propose to use your donations for missions or other vital works, sizable portions of donations received are used instead for palatial mansions, ranches, and a luxurious lifestyle which the average donor is totally unaccustomed to. Such is the result of blind devotion to Christian leaders.

When St. John fell at the feet of his interpreter and guide, he was rebuked in the following terms: "See thou do it not: I am thy fellowservant, and of thy brethren that have the testimony of Jesus: worship God" (Rev. 19:10). Such a sharp rebuke needs to be administered by Christian leaders to those of their followers who would worship them as some kind of minor deity.

Blind allegiance to human leaders will only lead to feuding and division among members of the body of Christ. Any such leader who will allow such folly when he has the responsibility to divert that devotion to Jesus, but will not because he loves the praise of men, is really no leader at all. Rather, he is a pompous, selfish, petty person who has, instead of mustard-seed faith, a mustard-seed ego. He is not a fiery Elijah; he is rather a sniveling, balking, bawling Balaam, powerless to bless or curse.

The Scriptures do teach us to give honour to whom honour is due. But let us keep it honour and not worship and devotion. Let us respect Christian leaders, but let us not worship them as though they can do no wrong.

Babylon

And after these things I heard a great voice of much people in heaven, saying, "Alleluia; Salvation, and glory, and honour, and power, unto the Lord our God."

REVELATION 19:1

This, the first hallelujah in the Book of Revelation is provoked by the total destruction and downfall of a city which is again and again described as "great." Why does heaven so exult at the overthrow of Babylon? Because Babylon embodies the spirit of empty show and pretense. Babylon speaks of that system of religion that is more interested in *pomp*, *pageantry*, and *pretense* than the souls of men. Such religions appeal to the showy, proud nature of men who desire repute and acclaim. Men will be religious and they will meet strict demands of religion if those demands fall within certain boundaries and are a means to obtain a certain goal. But these same men will rebel at the simple plan of God's salvation with simple demands of separation from sin.

Israel's first recorded sin after entering Canaan was the taking of a Babylonian garment. This garment was more than a piece of clothing. This garment represented the pomp and pageantry of vain religion. This could have been a garment that was worn by idol-worshippers. Whatever it was or represented, it was forbidden by God and that is enough.

The Babylonian spirit was found in the early church when Ananias and Sapphira chose to lie, desiring the acclaim of others for their great sacrifice, while making no sacrifice in giving at all.

The hosts of heaven will rejoice over the fall of Babylon; that great whore, guilty of the blood of saints. That should be enough said! We should be able to discern by that, that any leaning toward patterns of Babylonian ways, any tendency to a religion of pomp, pride and pretense, is detestable to our God.

Let us always remember that it is the humbling of ourselves under the mighty hand of God, that brings about exaltation. Let us recognize that when we truly humble ourselves under God's hand that we do not care if we are exalted or not. We are content to have His fellowship and the strength of His presence.

The Church doesn't need Pomp——
                    It needs Plainness.
The Church doesn't need Pride——
                    It needs Humility.
The Church doesn't need Pretense——
                    It needs Preciseness—Truth.
The Church doesn't need Pageantry——
                    It needs Piety—Holiness.

A Worker Approved

Study to shew thyself approved unto God, a workman that needeth not to be ashamed, rightly dividing the word of truth.

2 TIMOTHY 2:15

What is the basic difference in the church of today and the early church? Mainly this: human power is used to do divine work. We trust more in the greatness of men than the greatness of God. Every direction you turn, there is ever the encouragement to feed the intellect; to have the mind, so that you may be used of God. There is undeniably benefit in study and preparation. There is also danger; the danger lies in the tendency of men to become cocksure and overconfident, knowledgeable of the Word, but lacking an intimate relationship with the Author, the Lord Himself.

The truth is that in some instances we have wrongly interpreted Paul's instruction to Timothy to "study to show thyself approved"—approved unto whom? That is the question. The emphasis is wrongly placed at times, and many are made to feel that unless we have received a degree from a college or university, we will lack approval. No doubt we will be unapproved, but let men think what they will. It is the approval of God that we seek—and what value is all of our learning?—What value is all of the ability that we have developed, if it does not meet with God's approval? Oh, but you say, it must. Who is grading the test papers? Maybe you made straight A's, but who graded you? How would you rate if God were doing the grading? Rest assured, He is.

May God help us now. We have so long sought for the approval of men that we have forgotten to ask what our Father thought about us. How we need to wake up to the desire of the Holy Spirit! I do not speak of just a spiritual awakening, but rather an awakening to the Spirit, to the fact that it is the power of the Holy Spirit in us and working through us that anything worthwhile is accomplished. Too long we have moved in the direction of relying on the intellect, trusting and depending on men, wise and acclaimed by the world, but novices in spiritual matters.

Everything about the early church pointed to Christ and the power of the Holy Spirit upon men. The Council said, "are not these *unlearned* men?" Would not some unlearning be of great value today, if in the process we learned to completely depend on the Holy Spirit as Jesus told us to do?

Control

> This I say then, Walk in the Spirit, and ye shall not fulfil the lust of the flesh.
>
> GALATIANS 5:16

These are days when we have been told, "don't hold it in," "let it all out," "tell it like it is," throw self-control to the winds, forget about your inhibitions, and do what you feel like doing.

To many, this sounded like the perfect solution, until now we live in an age of uncontrolled and now uncontrollable passion. And now with the death penalty removed the Supreme Court for nearly all murder, rape, kidnapping, etc.—if you agree with the psychologists that this is not a deterrent to murder, you say that they are wiser than God—we can get ready for Paul's prophecy in 2 Timothy 3, concerning the perilous last days to come to pass in lurid color before our eyes.

But, thank God for control. Controlled by the Spirit, we shall not fulfill the lust of the flesh. Paul writes much about the Spirit-controlled life in Romans 8 also. In Romans 8:14, Paul writes, "For as many as are led"—controlled by the Spirit of God—"they are the sons of God." Now, a Holy Spirit-controlled man *needs no law to cause him to live a righteous life*. Galatians 5:22-23 speaks of the fruit of the Spirit—the fruit produced in a believer as a result of the Holy Spirit's control—and says, "against such there is no law." The fruit of the Spirit is love manifested (shed abroad in our hearts by the Holy Spirit, Rom. 5:5) in joy, peace, longsuffering, gentleness, goodness, faith, meekness, temperance:

1. Joy is love's strength.
2. Peace is love's security.
3. Longsuffering is love's patience.
4. Gentleness is love's conduct.
5. Goodness is love's character.
6. Faith is love's confidence.
7. Meekness is love's humility.
8. Temperance is love's victory. [1]

Let your rule be—*ruled by the Holy Spirit.*

A Mockery of Sin

Fools make a mock at sin: but among the righteous there is favour.

PROVERBS 14:9

Would you take a rattlesnake to bed with you? Would you play around with a poisonous viper? Would you walk along the top edge of the

---

[1] Porter L. Barrington, *Christian Life Bible*. Nashville: Thomas Nelson, 1985.

Empire State Building, mocking at the height? Would you walk the wings of an airplane in flight, defying death without a parachute? Would you play Russian Roulette (a game in which one shell is placed in a cylinder of a revolver and the the cylinder is twirled and then the pistol is placed to the forehead and the trigger pulled)?

You probably wouldn't think of doing any of these things. Yet there is another thing that is far more deadly than any of the above. The consequences are far greater, and they are eternal in duration. It is simply this: making a mockery of sin.

To mock is to ridicule, to jeer at, to make sport of. God said when a man treats sin as such, that man is a fool, for sin is never to be taken lightly. To break the powerful hold of sin upon man; it took the love of God, the gift of His Son. It took the agony of the cross, the Son giving His life; and it took the power of God, the resurrection of Jesus. How can we consider ourselves "smart" when we jeer at that which cost God so much to redeem and rescue us from?

Don't toy around with sin! What may start out as a harmless pastime, can end up in eternal heartache if the thing is done without regard to the Word of God or the will of God. We need to give due regard to the power of sin and its eternal consequences. Don't mock it!

Hitchhikers!

In our travels the past few months, I have had the opportunity on many occasions to view the many hitchhikers along the highways these days. Now people, especially men, have been hitchhiking for many years, but in the last few years the situation has certainly changed. There seems to be several points of similarity among hitchhikers today which I hope to relate to the spiritual life, for I feel that the church has its hitchhikers.

First of all, hitchhikers are usually vague concerning their destination. Some of them know where they want to go, but most are content just to be going in some direction. Now, there are those in the church today who know that they don't want to go to hell, but they are not excited about going to heaven.

Second, a hitchhiker is content to ride a short distance and will ride with anyone, in or on just about anything. Here, again, is an interesting parallel, for the church is plagued with those who will ride a short distance and then, when a tire blows out or the engine develops trouble, they're ready to desert you and hitch a ride with someone else.

Third, hitchhikers are people without much luggage; in other words, the hitchhiking

Christian is one without a burden. They won't accept the burden of service to the Lord such as teaching, praying, witnessing, etc.

Fourth, hitchhikers are generally indifferent about their personal appearance. Some of them are grotesque-looking creatures who are apparently boycotting soap and water. The Christian who has no regard for his personal appearance has no regard for others, and certainly no respect for the Lord or the church. We are Christ's ambassadors! Let us attire ourselves in an appropriate fashion; clean and modest, above reproach.

Fifth, hitchhikers are potentially dangerous. Many people have welcomed an individual into their auto, only to find out later that this person had a gun in their ribs and wanted their money, car and life. The person who has had trouble in another church sometimes can be deadly. If they attack the church they came out of, there is a good chance it will be us next.

To sum it all up, the Word instructs us not to be hitchhikers, but rather to drop the hitching a ride, and start hiking. Paul writes in Galatians 5:16, "walk in the Spirit, and ye shall not fulfill the lust of the flesh."

Abiding!

And now, little children, abide in him; that, when he
shall appear, we may have confidence, and not be
ashamed before him at his coming.

1 JOHN 2:28

Some people seem to be confused concerning
the doctrine of salvation and rewards. While
salvation is the gift of God and cannot be
earned, rewards are for labor (fruit-bearing of
John 15:1-6). However, the latter (reward for
fruit-bearing) is entirely dependent on the
former. There can be no fruit-bearing without
"abiding." And if we *abide* in *Him*, there can be
nothing else but *fruit* in our lives (John 15:5).

To abide in, is to the stand fast in, refusing to
be moved. If we abide in Christ and His words
abide in us, we have a divine guarantee of
answer to prayer. Jesus makes no provision for
the failure of His disciples. So if we fail, it is first
of all, "a failing to abide." If we stand fast in
Christ, John says we will not be ashamed at His
coming.

Who will be ashamed? Those who professed
to be abiding and were not—for those who know
them will then see through their shoddy
testimony. It is to your personal gain to take
inventory of your own experience. "Every
branch in me that beareth not fruit he taketh

81

away." (John 15:2) Notice that it is the husbandman, the Father, and not man, that takes away the branches that do not bear fruit.

In the Parable of the Talents, it is double or nothing. In John 15, it is bear fruit, or be taken away. There is no provision for failure, neither is there excuse. If we "abide," we shall "accomplish," and great will be the reward.

Whose Image?

"Tell us therefore, What thinkest thou? Is it lawful to give tribute unto Caesar, or not?"

But Jesus perceived their wickedness, and said, "Why tempt ye me, ye hypocrites? Shew me the tribute money." And they brought unto him a penny. And he saith unto them, "Whose is this image and superscription?"

They say unto him, "Caesar's."

Then saith he unto them, "Render therefore unto Caesar the things which are Caesar's; and unto God the things that are God's."

MATTHEW 22:17-21

Jesus used a penny with Caesar's image on it to teach men that it was lawful to pay taxes. However, in doing so, Jesus also taught a far more important lesson. Jesus taught in this example to render (give) unto God the things that are God's.

What few people realize is that God already has a claim on you. YOU ARE MADE IN THE IMAGE AND LIKENESS OF GOD! Whether we want to recognize this claim or not makes no difference. The fact of an accounting for every individual, a judgement day, emphasizes this claim. *You may not believe*, but *all* of your unbelief will not change the Word of God. Some men are ridiculous to the point of thinking because they do not believe in the existence of God, that He doesn't exist. To many in our world today, this is thought to be *wsdom*. These people who declare such are supposed to be people of greater intelligence. The Word of God declares them to be a fool! People with this same level of intelligence and degrees could also say there is no *sun*, and they might as well, for they would be just as correct as they are when they say "there is no God."

Perhaps there are a few things that we need to realize about the atheistic teachers that fill our classrooms today. First of all, we need to realize that because a man has a degree, it does not mean that he is a wise man; it could mean only that he has a good memory. Secondly, these people are not scholars in the Word of God.

How can you learn anything from a book you don't believe?

As Christians, we are to bear the image of the heavenly as we have borne the image of the earthy" (Rom. 15:49). "He that saith he abideth in Him ought himself also to walk, even as He walked" (1 John 2:6).

Divine ownership? Absolutely! Proof from both Testaments. "Behold, all souls are mine; as the soul of the father, so also the soul of the son is mine; the soul that sinneth, it shall die" (Ezek. 18:4). "Whether we live, therefore, or die, WE ARE THE LORD'S" (Rom. 14:8)!

Be Still & Know That I Am God

> Be still, and know that I am God: I will be exalted among the heathen, I will be exalted in the earth.
>
> PSALM 46:10

This command from the Old Testament seems to be totally contrary to the New Testament command of our Lord, "Go ye!" For instance, how can you "be still" and "go ye"? But the above command is twofold—"be still and know." There is no point in "going" if there is no "knowing" that He is God.

To "be still" speaks of cessation of our efforts. It is a call to "quit" the attempts made by the flesh to accomplish that thing that the Lord wills to do for us. It is a command to REST! REST in His power and in His faithfulness to do the impossible. It is a *teaching* command as well, for it teaches us that we can only really know God through "being still," or resting in His faithfulness. Our God is never in a hurry, yet He is never late; and while Jesus commands us to "go," He promises to go with us—not before us or behind us, but *"with us."* Realize now that in *going* He does not adopt our pace, but we adopt His; and He does not walk in our way, but here again, we walk in His way.

Followers or Besiders?

If we consider and obey this command with the additional illumination of New Testament revelation, then we understand that *we are not followers*, but rather *"besiders."* For one to be still and know (learn) that He is God (El Shaddai, Nourisher, Provider, our Everything) and then "go" with this knowledge as Jesus commanded, then we have the blessed experience of a "besider"—Jesus going with us. Consider now that Jesus' command and promise is conditional —"you go, and I'll go *with* you." In other words, if we're not going, we may be *followers*, but a long way off; for He is *with* those who are carrying out His command.

Certainly—"be still and know"—this is necessary, a must—but after you *know*—how in the world can you just sit there—knowing what you do?

Look at the rest of Psalm 46:10: "I will be exalted among the heathen; I will be exalted in the earth." Yes, You will, Lord, and I intend to be one of those "besiders," telling of Your goodness and mercy, shouting out praise unto You—going with the "Good News" of redemption for body, soul and spirit—going Your way at Your pace.

I challenge you: become a "besider."

Friends

"Greater love hath no man than this, that a man lay down his life for his friends. Ye are my friends, if ye do whatsoever I command you. Henceforth I call you not servants; for the servant knoweth not what his lord doeth: but I have called you friends; for all things that I have heard of my Father I have made known unto you."

JOHN 15:13-15

Abraham was the first mortal that God called His friend as far as we know from the biblical account, though there were many before Abraham that no doubt could have been considered worthy of such an honor. Enoch, for example, certainly was on such terms with God.

The word 'friend' means a person whom one knows well and holds affection for; a person on the same side in a struggle. Several things are generally common among friends. In others words, people usually become friends because of a common interest, an affection or love for something. Also, people become friends because they talk with one another. As strange as it may seem, often times people living in the same house and members of the same family are anything but friends. This is the common tragedy that blights America and the world today: members of the same household, but not friends.

Do you consider yourself a friend of God? Do you consider God as your friend? We often speak of the Lord as a friend that is closer than brother, but is He that to you? It was after three years of walking with His disciples that Jesus finally called them friends, and even then He made it quite clear that their friendship was based on obedience to His commands. The attitude of Christ toward friendship is not that of a domineering friend—no, never. It is rather the attitude of a friend who seeks only the best for us and knows that this can only be achieved by our following his instructions and commands to the letter. Also, James 4:4 states that to be a friend of (hold affection for) the world is to become God's enemy. Any love or fondness for the world is considered by God to be a breach of trust and a dissolving of friendship. True, in this, God assumes the role of a jealous friend, and that He is. When it comes to loyalty of affection, He makes it clear. He is a jealous God, but how we praise Him for this. He is jealous for our good. Our greatest enemy is the world, so God draws the line and says, "if you love the world, the love of God is not in you," and any friendship with the world is enmity against God. Plain, yes, but thank God, it leaves no room for debate or doubt. God seeks our good. He is willing to be our friend if we are. We prove our willingness by abandoning the world and submitting our will to obey His Word.

The Key to the 23rd Psalm

... for his name's sake.

PSALM 23:3

Four little words right in the heart of this psalm are the key to all that is promised herein. Let us review again the message of this psalm.

"The Lord (Jehovah, the Eternal One) is my Shepherd. I shall not want (therefore I lack nothing)."

"He maketh me to lie down in green pastures. He leadeth me beside the still waters." The reference is to a well-watered oasis of fresh green grass and restful water, a place of abundant supply. He makes me stop and feed in the quiet refreshing place. Perhaps we wouldn't stop, but He is our Shepherd, and He provides this rest and refreshing for us.

"He restoreth my soul"; and again as it is throughout the psalm, and throughout our experience, it is the Lord who is continually doing something for us.

"He leadeth me in the paths of righteousness"—and now we come to the key: the four words that say so much—"for His name's sake." This is the answer as to why the Lord is doing all this. It is not for my desert that He does it but for His name's sake. It is not for my honor, but for His honor.

He supplies my wants; He shepherds me; He leads me to the refreshing oasis of fresh grass and restful waters. He does what no earthly power can ever do. *He restores my soul.* He leads me in righteous paths for His name's sake. How we need to think on this! The paths of righteousness have been forsaken by so many in these times. Some would even make us believe that we really haven't been led by the Lord at all, but it is just convictions imposed by others. Let them say what they will; let others desert the paths of righteousness for the cheap and frivolous things of this world. Let us concern ourselves with being led, for His name's sake. Let us walk in the paths of righteousness that it may bring honor to God's name.

The rest of the benefits promised by the Lord in this psalm, i.e., freedom from fear; the comfort of His rod and staff; the anointing with the fresh oil of the Holy Spirit; the promise of goodness and mercy; and finally, reception into the eternal habitation of God, are all "for His name's sake." Certainly, we are the beneficiaries. But, thank God, it is because He has promised and because of His faithfulness, that we receive anything at all. We are redeemed, anointed, separated, not for our sakes, but for His name's sake. It is to the name of Jesus that every knee shall bow and every tongue confess: that He is Lord to the glory of the Father.

Love

"By this shall all men know that you are my disciples."

JOHN 13:35

Love—that distinctive power that comes into our lives when we receive Christ—that which is manifest by the Holy Spirit (Rom. 5:5)—is the peculiar trademark (identifier) of the church. Love for one another renders useless and unnecessary any and all use of other things in an attempt to achieve identity. Such things are senseless and a contradiction of the teachings of Jesus our Lord.

Love for one another is received not by striving or seeking for it, but rather by submission to our Lord and to the working of the Holy Spirit within us. Love for one another must be communicated, acted out, demonstrated, if it is to achieve its purpose in us. It cannot be kept secret. We must allow it to be known in the church, in the marketplace, in the world.

This love for one another that Jesus was speaking of knows no boundaries. Nothing can contain it! It breaks across all racial barriers, all cultures, all political or party differences; it ignores personality traits, is blind to short-comings and failures; it is oblivious to position, wealth (or lack of it), fame. Here in Trinity

Christian Center, this kind of love for one another is our chief pursuit.

A Thank-You

Thanks! We love you and we know that we are loved.

Your love, kindness and generosity to me and all of my family and guests will always be remembered by us. I simply cannot put into words our gratitude for the lovely meal that you prepared and served by family. Your expressions of sorrow and compassion greatly ministered to my spirit. I know also that I was strengthened through your prayers. Please continue to pray for my brother's wife and children as they face the aftermath of questions and grief resulting from his passing.

Failure & Shallowness of Experience

SEE MARK 4:1-20.

In the text, in Mark's Gospel, Jesus tells the parable of the sower that went out to sow. In verse 14, Jesus explains the parable thus: "The sower soweth the word." It is indeed a strange thing that the Word is spoken of as being the cause of failure and shallowness. Now, we have no right or desire to argue, but generally, a farmer or gardener feels the seed has certainly done its work if it breaks the ground and comes forth. However, this is not the case in this parable.

Two things we need to keep in mind: first, the Word is certainly unlike any other seed. Second, reaction to the product of the seed, for the Word produces in the life experience much more than fruit. The Word produces, before fruit is born, affliction and persecution. Jesus said these twins come for "the word's sake," or because the individual has receives the Word and accepted Christ. Notice also, that it is not these twins, affliction and persecution, that causes the failure and shallowness, but it is the fact that the person becomes offended by their visit. Since they are there because of the Word, the person ends up rejecting the Word, casting it aside in order to rid himself of these unwelcome visitors. I say they are visitors, for they will not be around always.

While the "stony ground" Christian's life ends in complete failure, the "thorny ground" Christian's experience ends in shallowness and unfruitfulness, which amounts to the same thing. Unfruitfulness results in one being cut off from the vine by the husbandman (the heavenly Father). (See John 15.)

Now in the case of the "thorny ground" Christian, he has three things that affect the outcome. These are things that he must impale upon the cross or the Word will be ineffective. The cares of the world, the deceitfulness of riches, the lusts of other things—this unholy threesome chokes the Word. What simply happens is that these enter in and create a conflict over the demands of Christ. Jesus said, "take up thy cross." These say, "Must I give up (surrender) everything?" Jesus says, "Come, follow me!" These three say, "you will be poor." "Deny thyself" is still the call, but the lusts of the other things say, "think of your home, your future, your family, all that you've worked for and all that you love." And so the Word is choked because of the recipient's refusal to deny himself.

It is ironic that the same Word that results in failure and shallowness also results in victory and spiritual depth. It is simply how we react to the Word. It comes down to the question of our willingness to totally surrender to the Word. Oftentimes, when a person doesn't want to be ruled by a certain portion of Scripture, he will start a question with these words: "Now, don't you think . . ." This is done sometimes in an attempt to evoke a compromise from the one preaching and teaching. But it takes no interpretation for what Jesus said when He cried, "If any man will come after me, let him deny himself and take up his cross, and follow me" (Matt. 16:24). Believe the Word; let the Scriptures be the rule of your life. Two plus two equals four; this is a mathematical fact leaving no room for debate or argument. Obedience and surrender to the Word equals victory and spiritual depth. This is an eternal fact.

Abiding in Christ

"Abide in me, and I in you. As the branch cannot bear fruit of itself, except it abide in the vine; no more can ye, except ye abide in me."

JOHN 15:4

Abiding simply means to remain, to continue, to dwell. Abiding in Christ is not something we need to work at, but simply rest in. We do not need to try to get in, for we are not told to *get into Christ*, but simply to *abide in Him*. For if we have been born again, we are in; it was not our action that put us there, but God's act. Ephesians 2:6 tells us we are raised in Him. Colossians 2:10 tells us we are complete in Him. Ephesians 1:3 tells us we are blessed with *all* spiritual blessings in Him. The entire work regarding us is done in Christ.

Abide in me and I in you—the "I in you" is the outcome of abiding in Him. We need to guard against being too anxious about the subjective side of things. We need rather to dwell upon the object—"abide in me." It is God's word to put us in Christ—in the place of abiding —it is our work to abide.

Abiding also speaks of sweet contentment. One is not apt to stay in a place long unless they are content to do so. So let us be content to just abide in Christ. He that abideth in me, and I in

96

him, the same bringeth forth much fruit. We cannot bear fruit by our labours. We bear fruit because of our abiding, by our staying put or in place, where God has placed us, in Christ. No fruit tree would ever bear fruit if it was transplanted, taken out of the soil and placed back in it every few weeks. Neither can the Christian bear fruit unless he abides in Christ.

In closing, let me say again: Do not concern yourself with bearing fruit; rather, concern yourself with abiding in Christ. God has put you in His Son; stay there and the rest will take care of itself.

A Lesson from Revelation

I was in the Spirit on the Lord's day, and heard behind me a great voice, as of a trumpet, saying, "I am Alpha and Omega, the first and the last": and, "What thou seest, write in a book, and send it unto the seven churches which are in Asia; unto Ephesus, and unto Smyrna, and unto Pergamos, and unto Thyatira, and unto Sardis, and unto Philadelphia, and unto Laodicea."

And I turned to see the voice that spake with me. And being turned, I saw seven golden candlesticks; and in the midst of the seven candlesticks one like unto the Son of man, clothed with a garment down to the foot, and girt about the paps with a golden girdle. his head and his hairs were white like wool, as white as snow; and his eyes were as a flame of fire; and his feet like unto fine brass, as if they burned in a furnace; and his voice as the sound of many waters. And he had in his right hand seven stars: and out of his mouth went a sharp two-edged sword: and his countenance was as the sun shineth in his strength.

And when I saw him, I fell at his feet as dead. And he laid his right hand upon me, saying unto me, "Fear not; I am the first and the last."

REVELATION 1:10-17

These are days of endless frustration, distress and unrest. The world is sick and troubled, and too many Christians are allowing the world's troubles to spill over onto them and blight their happy experience in Christ.

Also, many Christians today are carefully scrutinizing every world situation that may point to some fulfillment or possible fulfillment of Bible prophecy. There is an astounding interest in end-time prophecy. Authors have become wealthy writing their predictions of end-time events.

But read the above mentioned Scriptures and make a note of two very significant things.

One: John was in the Spirit on the Lord's Day. It was not anything unusual for John to be in the Spirit on this day or any other day, and a study of his life will certainly reveal this to be a true pattern of his life. But this reference points to the difference that living in the Spirit makes.

Two: Many look at the revelation as a revealing of events to come. John speaks of this in chapter one, verse one, as "the Revelation of Jesus Christ." Being in the Spirit, the first revelation John had was Jesus Christ in all his glory. John saw Christ, first and last. What is sandwiched in between the revelation of Christ in the first of the book and the last of the book is not the most important thing, although many have given great importance to these things sandwiched in between—so much importance, that many are more concerned about the Man of Sin than the sin of man. Many are more concerned about knowing who the Antichrist is than they are of knowing Jesus Christ as Paul sought to know Him.

Let us learn a lesson from John. . . . John, who had his troubles, banished to die of loneliness on a deserted island, cast out, rejected, persecuted, hated for Jesus' sake. John continued to live in the Spirit, and living in the Spirit, he saw none of his difficulties; he experienced no loneliness; he felt no rejection, for he saw Jesus. Let us learn to look away from the world beset with conflicts and look to Jesus. Allow Him to possess our vision. What's coming in the way of world trouble or events, is of little importance to the Christian. WHO is coming is the important thing to the Christian!

Christian Brotherhood

New Testament Commands Regulating Christian Brotherhood

SEE ROMANS 12:9-16

1. Let love be without dissimulation—not disguised, but real, evident, showing.
2. Abhor that which is evil—hate, detest, and loathe all evil.
3. Cleave to that which is good—be cemented or glued to the good.
4. Be kindly affectioned one to another—love with brotherly affection.
5. In honor preferring one another—Be forward to honor others.
6. Not slothful in business—Never be careless, lazy, indifferent.
7. Fervent in spirit—Boiling over with zeal for the Lord.
8. Serving the Lord—Put your life into God's service, whether or not you receive personal gain or applause.
9. Rejoicing in hope—Let your hope be a joy to you.
10. Patient in tribulation—Show patience and trust in God in all your trouble.
11. Continuing instant in prayer—Live in fervent prayer to God.

12. Distributing to the necessity of the saints—Contribute to needy saints, care about them as they are members of our family.
13. Given to hospitality—Make a practice of being hospitable.
14. Bless them which persecute you—Bless and pray for your habitual persecutors; love your enemies.
15. Rejoice with them that do rejoice—Take a lively interest in the blessings of others without grudging.
16. Weep with them that weep—Always show a genuine compassion for others.
17. Be of the same mind one toward another—Live in harmony and in one accord with others.
18. Mind not high things—Do not be unlawfully ambitious to be rich and powerful. Do not count the favor of rich and powerful men. Do not shun the poor.
19. Condescend to men of low estate—Associate with godly and humble people, going through life with as little show and parade as possible.
20. Be not wise in your own conceits—Put away self-conceit and vanity—we are nothing except what Christ has made us.

Happiness in Doing

"Verily, verily, I say unto you, The servant is not greater than his lord; neither he that is sent greater than he that sent him. If ye know these things, happy are ye if ye do them."

JOHN 13:16-17

As long as man exists, there will exist with him a search for happiness, for more than anything else in life, real happiness is the ultimate goal. I believe that first step to genuine happiness is to find Christ, to be "born again" and begin to live in the joy of sins forgiven. Many people have experienced this joy and peace and a few months pass and they find themselves lacking in the happiness department.

What is the reason? When they were first saved, they were overjoyed; they begin to study the Word and thrill at the wonderful discoveries of the Word, but now, they find themselves dragging into church, anxious for the service to be over. I think the answer is in the text—let us look at the promise and condition of happiness.

Jesus had just finished the Passover Feast with His disciples, and had risen from supper and took a towel and basin of water and began to wash the disciples' feet. After He had finished, He said, "I have given you an example, that you should do as I have done" (John ??). Now note the text that I have italicized, "If ye know these things." A lot of young converts are anxious to know all about the Word of God. (Thank God for this!) As a young Christian, I used to be thrilled by those who knew the Scripture well. (I still am!) It is a wonderful thing to have a great desire to know more—but *happiness comes not from knowing, but from doing.* You can make a study of the Scripture a lifetime occupation and never have the fullness of joy, or you can take to your heart the simple commands of Scripture, and in doing them, find the greatest happiness possible in this life.

For instance, I preached last Sunday morning that the church needs "helps." God has set "helps" in the church, and to help is to make it easier for something to happen. That we need those to work and pray in the altars, creating by prayer and praise an atmosphere where the seeker can easily get through to God—the Scripture teaches, that as pastor, I have rule over the church. The point is this: Those who obeyed that message, carried out my appeal, left the service Sunday night with joy overflowing. "Happy are ye if ye do them!"

An old Japanese Christian woman was disturbed by a thief breaking into her house. She saw he was desperately hungry, so she prepared him a meal. Then, in her simple and practical faith, she offered him the keys to her home. The man was so shamed by her action, and God spoke to his heart and he accepted Christ. A simply carrying out of Christ's command—"If your enemy hunger, feed him."

Happiness is not in knowing—though we need knowledge to do right. Happiness is in doing!

Cannibal Christians

But if ye bite and devour one another, take heed that ye be not consumed one of another.

GALATIANS 5:15

The one danger that faces every cannibal is that he may be captured and become the meal for other cannibals.

The Word says the same thing. If you are going to bite and devour, take heed that ye be not consumed also. The lesson here is simply this: if you become intent on destroying someone else; if by becoming a cannibal Christian you devour another, you simply confirm your backsliding and fall from grace.

It is like an old tale I heard one time. The fisherman was sitting on the bank, and off in the distance he noticed a snake on a log. When he glanced back a few moments later, there was another snake, smaller than the first one. The smaller snake started swallowing the bigger snake, but he couldn't quite get him down all the way. Then, as the fisherman watched, the bigger snake that was being swallowed by the little snake, turned, and started swallowing the smaller snake that was swallowing him.

About that time, the fisherman got a bite, and when he looked back, there was no sign of either snake. His assumption was that the big snake had swallowed the smaller snake that had almost swallowed him, and in doing so, the big snake had swallowed himself and so disappeared.

I know that's a ridiculous tale, but Paul writes of being consumed as a result of your own biting and devouring of another.

But there need not be any danger of this happening if we follow the injunction of verse 16 to "walk in the Spirit." Jesus said of the Holy Spirit, "He shall glorify me" (John 16:14). One cannot say, when he cuts his brother or sister down with the words he speaks, that he is speaking by the Holy Spirit. The desire or lust of the flesh is to always make ourselves look good and others to look bad or inferior; whereas the work of the Spirit is to enable us to walk in meekness, caring nothing for the praise of men, but exalting the Lord Jesus.

Remember, when you are gulping someone else down, that you are also being consumed. With every bite, there goes more of your victory, your faith, your salvation.

He Cometh!

> But when the fulness of the time was come, God sent forth his Son, made of a woman, made under the law …
>
> GALATIANS 4:4

When Jesus was born, Israel was a subject nation. The greatness of the kingdom was but a memory, and Abraham's seed paid taxes to a foreign emperor, Caesar. In those days, Rome ruled the world. While the people of God groaned under the heel of Roman oppression, God declared it to be the time for Christ to come. Regardless of appearances, everything was prepared. God so loved the world that He gave His Son that *whosoever*—— That word, *whosoever*, takes in the world, not just the tiny nation of Israel. So God permitted Rome to conquer the world, and Jesus Christ was crucified in the Roman Empire upon a Roman cross for the salvation of the world that Rome had conquered.

Rome's communications were good. Her roads and her ships went almost everywhere. Jews could come to Jerusalem at Pentecost, hear the gospel and carry it back home without having to cross hostile national boundaries. Because Rome ruled, the apostles were able to travel freely from city to city within the Empire, speaking to men of the Savior. The Book of Acts demonstrates the neutrality and fairness of the secular in that day. Paul the apostle used his Roman citizenship to great advantage again and again. Hallelujah! Rome, likened to a wild beast in some passages of Scripture, was tamed by the God who shuts the mouths of lions. Tamed for God's used.

So the world again is being arranged by our God for the Second Coming of Christ. The nations will be gathered as the Word has declared, and as we approach this time of commemorating our Lord's First Coming, the bright star of the blessed hope of His Appearing seems to loom upon the horizon.

He cometh!

Living

"… I am come that they might have life, and that they might have it more abundantly."

JOHN 10:10

There is a vast difference in the way a Christian and an unbeliever spend their lives. The unbeliever, for the most part, lives selfishly, only for himself; while the Christian lives the same days, months and years, living for his Lord. Since none of us live or die to ourselves, living should take on a new significance. The kind of living experience of a man like Dr. John Geddie. Dr. Geddie went to Aneityum in 1848 and lived for God there 24 years. On the tablet erected to his memory by the people of Aneityum, these words are found: "When he landed in 1848, there were no Christians. When he left in 1872, there were no heathen." Now, brother, that is living!

Paul, the apostle to the Gentiles, known in heaven and hell; working and living under the constant surveillance and buffeting of the devil; a man who went further with the Gospel than any other man in a lifetime, summed it up with these words: "For me to live is Christ, and to die is gain" (Phil. 1:21).

In our living, we touch other lives that are influenced by our attitudes toward life. Two things about the Christian really wake people up. Number one is the Christian's joy. The thing that continually perplexed and confounded the rulers and religionists in the days of the apostles was their joy. If they whipped them, they were happy; if they imprisoned them, they were happy; and when they threatened them with death, they were happy to be accounted worthy to die for their Lord. These were the "happiness people," and the born-again, Spirit-filled child of God is still happy.

Number two is the Christian power; instead of being ruled by circumstances, he rules. The Christian is in command! Not by or in his own power, but by the power and authority of his Lord.

The Scriptures teach us that we are living epistles [letters], "known and read of all men" (2 Cor. 3:2). When men read your life, what is the message they receive? Does the fact that "Jesus is Lord" stand out in bold type? Does a message of happiness, power and love come through so loud that difficulties and disappointments are completely blotted out? Or do you complain so much that those whom your life touches get the impression that God is a tyrant that forsakes and curses His own?

Jesus came to give us life, and give it to us He did. The early church was so full of this Christ-imparted life that nothing seemed to mar their joy. Let the last-day church experience the same. Let us "live" as Christ did, as the early church did, as Paul did, as Dr. Geddie did—then our living will not be in vain.

The Privilege Is Ours

"Go ye therefore, and teach all nations …"
MATTHEW 28:19

When Christmas comes, we always think of the angels announcing the birth of Christ with the words: "I bring you good tidings of great joy, which shall be to all people" (Luke 2:10). It was the angel's privilege and joy to announce the birth of Christ to a small band of shepherds watching over their flocks. But it is our privilege and joy to announce to the entire world, not only the birth, but the death, burial and resurrection of our Lord Jesus Christ.

Only two times in the Scriptures are the angels afforded this privilege of telling about Jesus. The first, we mentioned above, which took place before the inception of the New Testament church. The second time will come in the future after the church has been caught up to be with our Lord. Revelation 14:6-7 says: "And I saw another angel fly in the midst of heaven having the everlasting gospel to preach on the earth, and to every nation, and kindred, and tongue, and people, saying, 'Fear God, and give glory to him.'"

The greater privilege is ours: there is nothing to indicate the angels were witnesses in the way the church is or should be. They merely announced Christ's birth or the gospel. Being a witness speaks of a much closer association. We know Christ in the fellowship of His suffering; angels do not. We know the joy of consecration, dedication and worship. The angels know nothing about these things in the way we do. Witness also speaks of martyrdom. It is our privilege to die for our Lord.

The coming of Christ has afforded us this privilege. Let us dedicate ourselves this Christmas-time to the unfinished task of spreading the "glad tidings." The privilege is ours.

Thou Art Poor!

> Because thou sayest, "I am rich, and increased with goods, and have need of nothing"; and knowest not that thou art wretched, and miserable, and poor, and blind, and naked.
>
> REVELATION 3:17

Often times, our estimate of ourselves is oceans apart from Christ's estimate of us. This is certainly borne out in the above-mentioned passage. They thought themselves to be rich. Christ said, "thou art poor"—poverty-ridden.

Now, while there can be many reasons why one may be poor in material things, there is no reason whatsoever for anyone to experience poverty in spiritual things.

Poverty, as mentioned by Christ here, does not refer to a momentary lack, but to a *continuous lack* which was brought on by a failure to store those things that would eliminate poverty. "Man shall not live by bread alone, but by *every* word that proceedeth out of the mouth of God" (Deut. 8:3). The Word of God is bread for the soul that never grows old or stale. It is the failure to lay up in the storeroom of our hearts the precious bread of God that brings about poverty of soul. When there is a poverty of the Word, there is a departure from the Word and misplaced emphasis.

Paul, for instance, spoke of those who thought gain is godliness (1 Tim. 6:5), and we still have such with us today. Then there are those who want to measure spirituality by the yardstick of emotion. This, too, is error and speaks of poverty (continuous lack) of the bread of God.

No doubt, the reason for the Lord's strong indictment of the Laodiceans was simply due to the fact that they were absolutely without excuse. For instance, they said, "we are rich." Now, you don't become rich by indifference or slothfulness. It also takes some intelligence to become rich. They were successful in the material things of life, but unsuccessful in the spiritual because they failed to apply themselves. These same traits that produced riches in material things can also produce riches in the spiritual life. For while they were not indifferent or slothful (lazy) in business matters, they were in spiritual matters; and while they were wise business people, no doubt they failed to use their minds to seek out the unsearchable riches of Christ.

If there is poverty of soul today, it is just as inexcusable now as it was then. The answer, too, is still the same: "Buy of me." In other words, "do business with God—business according to His terms."

Confidence: Handle with Care

Cast not away therefore your confidence, which hath great recompence of reward.

HEBREWS 10:35

One minister described confidence as that element of trust that enables on to walk through the Red Sea after faith had provided a dry pathway. Confidence is such a wonderful thing when it is rightly placed that the writer to Hebrews exhorts us to "handle it with care." Take care of confidence; don't carelessly throw it away.

How can one "throw away his confidence?" Well, he may throw it away on an unfaithful person as Proverbs has said: "Confidence in an unfaithful man in time of trouble [is like] a broken tooth, and a foot out of joint" (25:19). Picture, if you can, a man in that condition offering any help. He can't run to your rescue, his foot is out of joint; so, there he sits, trying to hold his head and his foot at the same time. He can't pray for you; he can't stand the air to hit the exposed nerve in that broken tooth. Don't throw away your confidence by placing it in an unfaithful person. Faithfulness is one thing that every Christian can attain. Moreover, it is required in stewards, that a man be found faithful. (See 1 Cor. 4:2.)

114

Confidence and trust in man is cursed by God in many instances. "Cursed be the man that trusteth in man, and maketh flesh his arm, and whose heart departeth from the Lord" (Jer. 17:5). When you come to the place that you have confidence in yourself or in others, that you can make it without God's help, you no longer lean on Jesus, nor trust in His mercy and grace; you have departed from the Lord and you come under the curse again. But "blessed is the man that trusteth in the Lord, and whose hope the Lord is" (Jer. 17:7).

Confidence has a great and eternal reward; handle it with care.

Trademarks

From henceforth let no man trouble me: for I bear in my body the marks of the Lord Jesus.

GALATIANS 6:17

A trademark is a symbol, word, letter or something that is used by the manufacturer to distinguish his products from those of his competitors. Man started using these as crafts developed, and craftsmen began to compete for customers. Trademarks are now generally registered with the government, and it is illegal for anyone else to use the trademark that belongs to another company or individual.

Paul, the apostle of the Lord, writes of "bearing in my body the *marks* of the Lord Jesus." He writes in 2 Corinthians 3:18 of "beholding the glory of the Lord" and that we are "changed into the same image." I remember the words of an old song that went, "I am marked, marked, marked." Yes, we have a mark upon us. It is not the mark of a letter, symbol or such thing, but it is the mark of the new birth and the seal of the Spirit.

The heart of the Gospel is change! The mark of the new birth is change! The trademark of the Christian indicates new owner! The marks on Paul's body testified to the ownership of the Lord Jesus. Let's tell it like it is! If you didn't experience change, you didn't experience the new birth!

In the new birth, there is the mark of separation. Old things pass away, and all things are become new. In this wonderful experience, we, like the prodigal son, give the pigs a permanent wave, and begin our journey home, loving the things we once hated, and hating the things we once loved.

There is the mark of the seal of the Spirit, which speaks of divine ownership. I mention again the fact that Christ means "anointed."

Jesus Christ means: Jesus, the Anointed. They were called Christians first at Antioch. My contention is this: that the word Christian means certainly to be Christlike, but in calling the church at Antioch 'Christians,' they were calling them 'the anointed ones.' This is borne out further by the fact that Christ was anointed, and how can you and I be Christlike without being *anointed?*

Yes, we are marked! Marked by the new birth; marked by separation; marked by the anointing; marked by love; marked by His peace; marked by joy in tribulation. God will have no problems distinguishing His people from an unholy and unregenerate world, for we bear in our bodies *his trademark.*

Trust & Obey

Yea, they turned back and tempted God, and limited the Holy One of Israel.

PSALM 78:41

One of the common mistakes of men today is limiting God. It seems that we cannot learn from others the loss involved when we stop trusting. God has not limited himself in meeting our faith for "*all* things are possible to him that believeth." The problem which generally arises is that we start trying to attend to God's business. It is God's business to answer our prayer, to confirm the Word with signs following, to astound men with the miraculous. However, too often we find ourselves fretting about the answer; and when we sweat about the answer, God just lets us sweat it out.

So why not let God attend to the business of answering, and you and I attend to the business of asking, believing, and living in expectancy of receiving the answer God has promised?

> Trust and obey,
> For there's no other way,
> To be happy in Jesus,
> But to trust and obey.

Past Feeling

... Who being past feeling have given themselves
over unto lasciviousness, to work all uncleanness
with greediness.

EPHESIANS 4:19

Feeling is a wonderful thing! Given due
consideration and understanding, we can say,
"Pain is a wonderful thing!" Pain may become
unbearable at times, but God in His wisdom
created our bodies and nervous systems to pain
us in certain situations. Now, we all think of
heaven as a place "free from pain," and no
doubt, it will be. But, as long as we remain here,
we need to feel pain once in a while.

We need to feel pain in order to really
appreciate the cross! We need to feel pain that
we may have compassion on others who are in
pain. However, God gave us a body capable of
pain for a far greater reason. That reason being,
to telegraph to the brain through the nervous
system that there is something wrong with the
part of the body that is hurting. If God had not
built this into the body, we would be endlessly
injuring, breaking or burning ourselves without
realizing anything was wrong.

Being without feeling is dangerous to the
spiritual man as well. Paul writes of those being
past feeling, no longer feeling any guilt or

119

condemnation of sin, giving themselves up to all kinds of wickedness. Not feeling guilt about a thing does not always mean it is approved by the Lord! Perhaps you have desensitized your spiritual man by a casual and continual disregard of the Word of God. Remember this! If it is condemned in the Word, it is sin regardless of how you may "feel" about it.

The writer of Hebrews tells us that we should, in the last days especially, give heed to church attendance. Now, there is more involved in this than just the need of fellowship. The greater reason, I believe, is the necessity of putting ourselves in a place where the Word of God can make us sensitive to the sin around us and the fact of Jesus' soon coming. Otherwise, how can we be sure we are looking and hasting unto His appearing? You may not "feel" He could come today—but then, you could be "past feeling!"

Out of Orbit

Raging waves of the sea, foaming out their own shame; wandering stars, to whom is reserved the blackness of darkness for ever.

JUDE 13

'Wondrous' is a word often used to attempt to describe the beautiful order God gave to the universe and all His Creation. Everything has its place! Stars have their orbit in which to move; the moon, reflecting the light of the sun, moves in its orbit around this earth, affecting tides and seasons.

The church has its order, too. Paul spoke of the resurrection thus: "Every man in his own order" (1 Cor. 15:23). When we mention order, we are not speaking of drab formality or death by ritual, but rather the order of the body which is used to describe the union of the church with Christ and each of us as "members in particular" (1 Cor. 12:27)

Jude speaks of those who despise dominion, and speak evil of dignities, who have gone in the way of Cain (self-righteousness) as "wandering stars," people who are *out of orbit*, out of the will of God, out of the body of Christ, denying God and our Lord Jesus. Jude tells us an awful lot in his brief letter; 1900 years ago, he told us space was black, but we didn't discover this until a few

121

years ago. But to *stay in orbit*, keep our place, lest we become as a wandering star, moving through the blackness of eternity without Christ.

Your position in Christ is important to you and to others. Keep it, move in the will of God, let Him direct your paths, lest you gravitate to the world and sin and slip "out of orbit."

Making Our Time Count

And whatsoever ye do in word or deed, do all in the name of the Lord Jesus, giving thanks to God and the Father by him.

COLOSSIANS 3:17

Paul must have been a very strict disciplinarian, ever conscious of the importance of using time for the work of Christ. The greatest failure of most Christians in these days is the failure to wisely and discretely make use of time.

It is important to note that this verse is sandwiched between the duties of Christians to others and the duties of Christians to relatives. Is it not true that much of the tension and strife that is generated in the home is due to the misuse of time and carelessness of activities— wives letting cooking and housework go while talking hours on the telephone; husbands slouching in an easy chair before a TV set with no time for the children?

And what about the Christian's duties to others? It is our duty as Christians to be merciful, kind, humble, meek, longsuffering, forbearing, and forgiving; putting on love, the bond of perfection, letting the peace of God *rule* (control) our hearts, teaching and admonishing (not talking about or discouraging) one another in psalms, hymns and spiritual songs.

Can we justify our actions, our words or deeds, as done in the name of the Lord Jesus? Can anyone justify endless (seemingly) telephone chatter which neither teaches, admonishes or edifies as words spoken in the name of the Lord? Can we waste time as though we have a million tomorrows in which to work for God, and then justify this waste in the light of eternal, never-dying souls lost in sin? Is it not also true that the tension, strife and division that develops among Christians is because of failure to heed and obey this passage of Scripture? Careless use of time leads to careless talk and careless actions.

May God use this passage to have a mighty impact upon us, that we may be more diligent, more faithful in the discipline of our time, our words and deeds, that they may bring honor to our Lord Jesus and eternal rewards to us.

Love Not the World

> Love not the world, neither the things that are in the world. If any man love the world, the love of the Father is not in him.
>
> 1 JOHN 2:15

It is not easy to define the word 'world,' for it covers a large scope. The Scripture speaks of the "prince of this world" (John 12:31), "the course of this world" (Eph. 2:2), "the god of this world" (2 Cor. 4:4), "the spirit of the world" which is contrary to the Spirit of God (1 Cor. 2:12), "the fashion of this world which is passing away" (1 Cor. 7:31) and "the wisdom of this world" which crucified the Lord of glory (1 Cor. 2:6).

There are people who are not worldly-minded, who are "laying up in store for themselves a good foundation against the time to come, that they may lay hold on to eternal life" (1 Tim. 6:19).

But *are you* the victim of worldliness? What "things" do you put first in your life? God is a jealous God who will "have none other gods before him." To what things are you passionately attached? The love of the dance? The show? The theater? Are you under the spell of politics, business power, science, money, ambitions, social popularity, worldly pleasures? Perhaps it's your pride in your home, your car, that boat?

You cannot hide your affection; though worldly passion be not apparent to other people, God knows! "For the Lord seeth not as man seeth; for man looketh on the outward appearance, but the Lord looketh on the heart" (1 Sam. 16:7).

Remember, worldliness is deadly. It is the white ant which eats away the frame of the "spiritual house." The apostle did not say, "love it not *too much*," or "love it not *so much*"; he simply says, "love it *not at all!*" Love not the world!

"Ye Have Heard"

Ye have heard that it was said of them of old time … but I say unto you …

MATTHEW 5:21-22

The people in Christ's day were in double bondage—bondage to Rome and bondage to the Law. Both Rome and the Law were constantly pointing an accusing finger—imagine, if you can, the pressure of living under this.

The Law was a standard of living, but it was a fixed standard. It was a rigid, inflexible code, not subject to adjustment, and leaving no room for advance beyond a given point. Jesus confronted the Law with these words: "But I say unto you." The words of Jesus contain a principle for all time; the principle of life; the principle of daily leading by the Holy Spirit. If I do the same thing the Lord led me to do a month ago because He speaks to me to do so again, that is life. But if I do it because He led me to do it a month ago, if I do it without that fresh assurance that He would have me do so, then that can become as binding as the Law of the Old Testament.

Now, I am writing about a spiritual walk—walking and living in the Spirit, moving daily under His direction. Remember also that the Spirit never leads us contrary to New Testament teaching. The New Testament is filled with life. It never takes us back under the bondage of the Law, but points to our deliverance in Christ. Notice Acts 15:24, where the council of the church writes to the Gentile church saying simply, "You are not under the Law," and anyone who tells you that we said you were is a subverter of the truth.

While the New Testament is filled with many commands, the difference in the Testaments can be found in two words: life and death. The Old Testament had its sentence of death. The New Testament has its sentence of life. Jesus said, "I've come that you might have life and life more abundantly." They didn't have life in the rigid code of Old Testament Law. If they did, then why these words from Jesus?

Thank God, we don't have to lie under the accusing finger of the Law, pointing to all our failures, but we live looking to the open arms of our Lord, saying, "Come unto me, come unto me and live," embracing us with love, clothing us in mercy. I live the way I do, not because of the Law, but because of the living Christ who daily leads me into the blessed experience of living in His presence. I preach because He has called, certainly, but also because I want to—I love to. I go to church because I love to, it's life to me. I tithe and give because I love to. I do none of these things because the Law says I must, but because Jesus gave me life, and is giving me life; He gave me love, and love is the fulfilling of the Law.

"He That Dwelleth"

> He that dwelleth in the secret place of the most
> High shall abide under the shadow of the Almighty.
>
> PSALM 91:1

The object of temptation by the enemy is always to get us to do something. To get us to move out of our coveted position in Christ is the whole purpose.

The following story is told about the last war between China and Japan. During the early months of the war, China had lost a considerable number of tanks to the Japanese and found themselves unable to deal with the Japanese armor—until the following scheme was devised. The Chinese placed snipers in strategic positions in ambush. When a Japanese tank appeared and came in range, the sniper would fire a single shot at the tank. After a considerable lapse of time, the first shot would be followed by a second; then further silence; then another shot, and on and on, until the tank driver, eager to locate the source of annoyance, would pop his head out to look around. The next shot, carefully aimed, would put an end to him. The whole scheme was devised to bring him out in the open.

In the same way, Satan's temptations are designed to entice us to expose ourselves, to step out of our hiding place. For he knows full well as soon as we move from the cover of Christ and act in self, he has scored a victory.

So don't let the little pings of caliber temptations draw you from your place in Christ. Certainly the devil knows how to time temptation so as to snare us. But let me close, calling attention to the fact that God knows how to keep us also. Stay hid with Christ in God.

What Shall We Say?

What shall we then say to these things? If God be for us, who can be against us?

ROMANS 8:31

This is God's promise of victory over every opposing force. The writer goes a little further in verse 37 of the same chapter to tell us we are *more* than conquerors through Him that loved us. To teach that there will not be opposition would be false, for the same word teaches that opposition will come—"all that will live godly in Christ Jesus shall suffer persecution" (2 Tim 3:12).

Now, the opposing forces of hell are an established fact, both in the Word and in our lives. But the promise of God, Himself promising the least of His saints and *all* of His saints, is victory over every foe.

Christ triumphed over every foe . . . death, hell and the grave. He is the Head; we are the members of His body.

Victory is inherent; we are His heir. Victory is ours. Believe it, confess it, shout it. We have overcome by His blood and the word of our testimony (our confession). We are more than conquerors through Him that dies for us.

What Are They Among So Many?

"There is a lad here, which hath five barley loaves, and two small fishes: but what are they among so many?"

JOHN 6:9

It seems that as the disciples were, so are we. They failed to look beyond the little lad's lunch to Jesus. It certainly was not because they had never witnessed a miracle, because Jesus had worked many miracles before now. It just seems to be a bent of our human nature to center our hopes on the state of our bank account rather than on the Lord's ability to bless.

It was the Lord who asked of Moses, "What is that in thine hand?" The answer, of course, was "a rod." A shepherd's staff, inexpensive and crude, but God showed Moses how that rod could be used as an instrument to bring about the deliverance of Israel.

What we have in our hands is so pitifully small that we are often hesitant to present it to the Lord for His use. But look beyond the smallness of what you have, to the bigness of Jesus.

No matter how much we possess, if it lacks the blessings of our Lord, it can never satisfy the hungry souls around us. All of the abilities that men may possess can never do what the touch of Jesus can do. How we need to realize this! Two hundred pennyworth seemed to be all the money the disciples had, but all they had would not meet the need. Everything we may try in the flesh will fail—utterly fail to satisfy the souls of men. We do not possess enough within ourselves to bless; we must have His touch and His touch alone.

It is said of Joshua and Caleb that they saw the giants, certainly, but standing taller than the giants was the promise, God's promise to give to them the land. Faith never denies facts, but it doesn't choke to death on facts either. Faith looks to the supreme eternal fact that not one of God's promises has ever failed.

What are these among so many? Not nearly enough, until Jesus takes it.

Christianity's Most Fundamental Question

> And when they were come to Capernaum, they that received tribute money came to Peter, and said, "Doth not your master pay tribute?"
>
> He saith, "Yes." And when he was come into the house, Jesus prevented him, saying, "What thinkest thou, Simon? of whom do the kings of the earth take custom or tribute? of their own children, or of strangers?"
>
> Peter saith unto him, "Of strangers."
>
> Jesus saith unto him, "Then are the children free. Notwithstanding, lest we should offend them, go thou to the sea, and cast an hook, and take up the fish that first cometh up; and when thou hast opened his mouth, thou shalt find a piece of money: that take, and give unto them for me and thee."
>
> MATTHEW 17:24-27

It was when they arrived in Capernaum that the question arose, "Doth not your master pay tribute?" The tribute money in this passage was a tax for the Temple. Jesus, evidently knowing the question in the mind of Peter, asked him,

"What thinkest thou, Simon? Of whom do the kings of the earth take taxes, of their own children or strangers?" Peter said, "of strangers."

The reason for the question in Peter's mind was this: Lord, you pay the tax or tribute, and so do we, but why? You're Lord of the Temple that the tax is levied against, and we're Your disciples. So why should we have to pay?

The answer as to why Jesus paid is in verse 27: " . . . lest we should offend them." In this answer, we are taught another great principle of Christianity. Even when our privileged position sets us free from certain obligations, we may have to forego our privileges for the sake of others, lest we become a stumbling block.

Anyone who finds himself unwilling to abide by the above needs to carefully examine his position in Christ, for such an attitude is totally unlike Christ. Is it possible to have Christ and be so unlike Him? Think for a moment of what Christ surrendered, all that He was willing and did forego for you and me. He had no obligation to pay tribute, for He was Lord; but, being Lord, He showed us a pattern. Let us follow in His footsteps.

Dead or Alive?

And you hath he quickened, who were dead in trespasses and sins.

EPHESIANS 2:1

A man is either quickened and alive, or he is not. There is no middle ground, no half-dead and half-alive, no half-saved and half-lost.

Death is a state of separation. Every dead one has been cut off from the power and source of life. The spiritual dead are cut off by their sins from the sustaining presence of God.

Death is a state of insensibility. The dead are neither charmed or alarmed by anything said or done in their presence. They have neither tears nor fears. Regardless of what happens, they remain expressionless.

Death is a state of helplessness and incapacity. We never expect anything from the dead. The dead have nothing in common with the living. *Who wants fellowship with a dead man?* Men dead in sins are out of communion and fellowship with God.

YOU HATH HE QUICKENED! Life is the only remedy for death. Religious form and ritual just dresses up the corpse. There must be an impartation of the quickening power of God to bring life.

Quickening brings SEPARATION! When Lazarus received life, he soon got out of the place of the dead. No living person in his right mind wants to live in a graveyard. Separation and change mark the man that has received the new birth and the Spirit baptism. It is difficult for me to believe that anyone quickened by the power of the Holy Ghost can be satisfied living among and fellowshipping with the dead.

Quickening produces CONSECRATION! This new life is to be "all for God." We are "quickened together with Christ." He has given life to me, can I do less than glorify Him through consecration for this life?

A Light Is a Light

"Ye are the light of the world. A city that is set on an hill cannot be hid."

MATTHEW 5:14

Does a light cease to be a light when it is out? Is a candle not a candle when it is not burning? Is a Christian no longer a Christian when he no longer gives witness (light) to the world?

Debate and argument about the above questions is vain and accomplishes nothing.

However, let me point out a few facts. All of the above were created to perform a certain function. Now, all arguments about these come to an end when they fail to function. For instance, Jesus said, "Ye *are* the light of the world." Now, He didn't say, "You may be the light of the world" or "you can be" or "you should be" or "you will be." No! Simply and surely, "Ye are the light!"

The single distinguishing factor that separates the Christian from the world more than anything else is the fact that a Christian shines . . . gives light (witness), showing the way to lost men.

Now, the world is filled with darkness, and who can deny it? But in this world of darkness, who will know one is Christian unless he shines forth? In Revelation, the testimony is that these saints overcame by the blood of the Lamb *and* the word of their testimony (witness).

It is not a matter of what you should be! Jesus said, "ye are," and if "ye are," "ye are" and if "ye are not," "ye are not"; and all the senseless debate will settle nothing.

Do a little checking! Are you performing that function for which you were created? Are you a light that never shines? A candle that never burns? A Christian that never gives witness?

In Matthew 13:43, Jesus speaks of that time when the righteous shall shine forth as the sun in the kingdom of their Father. Shining forth, radiating, reflecting the love and glory of God, is, and always will be, the Christian's identity. Yes, a light is a light, and regardless of what we may call it, it is not a light unless it is a light shining in darkness.

The Lord Is My Shepherd

The Lord is my shepherd; I shall not want.

PSALM 23:1

This psalm is the most beautiful passage in Scripture. But it goes far beyond just being a beautiful piece of literature often quoted by man. First of all, there is not *one* negative statement in this psalm. Secondly, it covers everything pertaining to the needs of mankind. Think of all the things that men strive and search for in this life, never quite attaining them because they trust in their own strength rather than to trust in God.

The eternal God is my Shepherd; I shall not want! I shall not want for:

Rest — for He maketh me to lie down in green pastures.

Refreshment — He leadeth me beside the *still* waters.

Forgiveness — for He restoreth my soul.

Companionship — for He leadeth me (walks along with me as my guide) in the paths of righteousness for His name's sake. Though I walk through the valley, I will not fear, for *Thou art with me!*

Comfort — for Thy rod and Thy staff, they comfort me.

Sustenance — Thou preparest a table before me in the presence of mine enemies.

Joy — Thou anointest my head with oil; my cup runneth over.

Anything in this life — Surely goodness and mercy shall follow me all the days of my life.

Anything in the life to come — for I will dwell in the house of the Lord forever.

Perfection!

Jesus said unto him, "If thou wilt be perfect, go and sell that thou hast, and give to the poor, and thou shalt have treasure in heaven: and come and follow me."

MATTHEW 19:21

Nobody's perfect! Now, I beg to differ with you. Somebody is perfect, not because they think so, but rather because they live so. I am speaking

138

from the standpoint of BIBLICAL PERFECTION and not that imagined human perfection that exists in the minds of so many.

First of all, we are commanded to be perfect. "Be ye therefore perfect, even as your Father which is in heaven is perfect" (Matt. 5:48). I believe some people do keep His commandments, and in doing so, they attain to Scriptural perfection.

Secondly, Jesus said in the verse that I gave for a text for these remarks, "If thou wilt be perfect, go and sell what you have, and give to the poor, and come follow me." "The young man went away sorrowful because he had great possessions" (19:22).

Now, perfection is not accomplished by giving away everything that you own; but rather perfection is attained by purging the heart and life of every single thing that would come between us and our Lord. The young man was sorrowful not because he had to be, but because he refused the joy of perfection in God by refusing to dispose of his wealth and follow Jesus.

Paul writing to the Philippians says, "I press toward the mark for the prize of the high calling of God in Christ Jesus. Let us therefore, as many as be *perfect*, be thus minded" (3:14). Perfection in one's life, according to Paul, involves the total abandonment of oneself to Christ, continually pressing toward the mark. It involves one motive, and that is to more fully do the will of God.

James, writing of the human tongue, says that any man who does not offend in word, or with the tongue, is a perfect man, and able also to control the whole body. We dare not disagree with this.

Finally, we are made perfect in love (1 John 4:18). First John has a wealth of instruction on love—read it. Love is the message that you heard from the beginning; the one message above all others that Jesus left His disciples. There is no perfection without love; neither is there any righteousness without love for your brother.

Pentecost

And when the day of Pentecost was fully come, they were all with one accord in one place.

ACTS 2:1

'Pentecost' is the one single word that throughout the years has indicated a significant spiritual experience. As on the day of Pentecost in Acts 2:1, it has created a hunger in many hearts and caused criticism to spring forth from others.

But as it was then, so is it even now. There were those who misunderstood the moving of the Holy Spirit. Today, there are many who only know what they have been told about the Pentecostal experience. There are those who simply do not understand our mode of worship, and the mistake many make is to simply rely upon what someone has told them about us, rather than investigate themselves. We readily admit that our services are different. There is rejoicing, there are testimonies, there are healings. Often there is the spiritual mani-festation of tongues and interpretation; also prophecy and other gifts of the Holy Spirit are manifested in the services. All of the above take place with one aim, to lift up the Lord Jesus Christ in our midst.

Now a new day has dawned. They talk about Pentecost in nearly every denominational circle. I have introduced myself as the pastor of a First Pentecostal Church and had Catholics ask me about the Pentecostal experience. Talk about Charismatic renewal all you want to, but when people attempt to identify Charismatic renewal with a church, who do you think they single out? The Pentecostal church, of course. Hungry hearts from all walks of life are seeking a deeper spiritual experience. Businessmen, affluent families, college students and graduates, teenagers, working men and women are developing a hunger for the precious gift of the Holy Spirit, and how we praise God for it.

The Day of Pentecost is here again! If you have not received this precious gift, let us know. Call or if you live out of the city, drop us a line, if you wish. We will pray with you and help you in any way we can. We will also send you, free of charge, tracts and books on the Pentecostal experience.

Appropriation & Substantiation

Now faith is the substance of things hoped for, the evidence of things not seen.

HEBREWS 11:1

These are two words important to every Christian who seeks to understand more fully his or her relationship to Christ and the Word. To appropriate means to take for one's own use. To substantiate means to show to be real or true by giving evidence; to prove, to give substance to. "Faith is the substantiating of things hoped for" (Heb. 11:1, DARBY) So then, faith is the proving of things hoped for.

By means of our senses, we substantiate facts in the natural realm. For instance, by the sense of hearing, I substantiate music. If I were deaf, then I would lack the full enjoyment of music, but the reality of music is unaffected by my ability or inability to hear it. So, if I lack the faculty to hear, it is as though music and sound never existed; my life is unaffected by it because I lack the faculty needed for its substantiation.

Now, the promises of God must be appropriated by faith. But facts are facts whether we believe them or not. If we do not believe the facts of the cross, they still remain as real as ever, only they are valueless to us. Faith does not make them real. They *are* real, but faith substantiates them and makes real in our life.

To further point out the difference between appropriation and substantiation, let us go to the Old Testament—Numbers 13. The children of Israel had been *promised* Canaan. Ten spies said there were giants there, and "we were in our own sight as grasshoppers" (Num. 13:33). The other two, Caleb and Joshua, did not deny facts (the giants), but confessed the promise, saying "we are able to take the land"—or, really, they said, "let us appropriate this land by faith, for God has promised."

Now the cross is a fact. Christ is seated at the right hand of God, making intercession for His saints, and that's a fact. The Holy Spirit has come in all His fullness, and that's a fact. Now, promises can become facts in one's life, depending on our ability to appropriate by faith, but facts remain facts. "He (Christ) abideth faithful; He cannot deny Himself" (2 Tim. 2:12).

Facts must be substantiated in our life by faith. The cross is a fact, but my life is only affected by the power of the cross when I believe and accept what Christ has done for me, when I die with Him on the cross and allow Him to live in me. You see, the fact of the cross is not proved to me or others in the world by the pages of historical documents. The proof of the cross is found in the millions of people whose lives have been changed by the power of the blood of the cross. The heathen are not convinced by words today anymore than they were in Paul's day, but they are convinced when they see evidence of the supernatural power of God being manifested through the life of a simple believer, whose only credentials are those of one who has sub-stantiated the cross, and is now appropriating the promise.

Divine Order

"But seek ye first the kingdom of God, and his righteousness; and all these things shall be added unto you."

MATTHEW 6:33

There must be order to our lives, and the proper order for the Christian is spelled out in the above text. This same plan for the life of God's child is reiterated over and over again in the New Testament. For instance, it emerges in the "model" prayer, often called "the Lord's Prayer." ("Our Father which art in heaven, Thy kingdom come, Thy will be done.")

The divine order is mentioned again by Jesus in His words to us. "If any man will be my disciple, let him deny himself, take up his cross, and come follow me."

That is divine order: to seek the kingdom of God first is to deny self. The natural way is for us to seek our own welfare first, but Jesus said to place the welfare of the kingdom of God first. As I mentioned last week, the kingdom is more than the King. The kingdom is the King plus the subjects, which in this case are those called out of sin from every tribe and tongue.

First things first—the kingdom of God *and* His righteousness (His justice, His equity). The righteous-ness of God was displayed by giving

Christ, His Son, to die not just for one nation, but for every nation. There is no inequity or injustice in the plan of redemption for man. Men who complain about injustice and inequality should come to Christ, for there are no inequities in Him.

This same divine order was mentioned again by Jesus in the Great Commission. There is absolutely no way that this command can be carried out without one first denying self.

Also, if we seek God's righteousness, then we must of necessity seek to achieve an equality in our ministry and outreach. We should seek by God's help to give as much for missions as we give for ministries at home. Perhaps we can't achieve this now, but we can seek. This is what Jesus said for us to do: *seek*—set a goal to work towards. With this promise, as we seek God, God will add. He will add (give freely) those things that others seek for. The word 'add' leaves no implication of striving for, or earning. God adds it to us, no strings, no sweat, no tension. That is the way of divine order.

Turn it around, and you'll have problems—real problems. Establish your life on the divine order, and you will be blessed—and men will call you blessed.

Will It Be Just Another Year?

I press toward the mark for the prize of the high
calling of God in Christ Jesus.

PHILIPPIANS 3:14

Many of us just closed out the old year and
began the new with a time of consecration and
dedication of ourselves to Christ. Perhaps you
may be one of those who were not satisfied with
your performance as a Christian in 1972. Well,
there is one thing for certain: 1973 will see no
better performance unless we sincerely desire it
and earnestly solicit the Lord's help and power
in our lives.

It is wonderful to make consecrations. It is
more wonderful to fulfill the task we have
consecrated ourselves to. Often when we are
worshipping in the sweet presence of God, it is
easy to say, "I'll go, Lord—here am I, send me."
Later on, we find it is easy to say and difficult to
follow through. I am not being critical of such
times. I only desire to encourage you by telling
you that "the will of God is not very often easy."
Paul said, "I press toward the mark." We have
set a goal, a mark to shoot at in consecration.
Now, if Paul had to "press," there was
opposition. He had to press, so to attain the goal
was difficult. The Christian life has *never* been
without opposition, and *never* will be.

It also seems the more determined we are, the more determined the opposing powers of darkness. But press on!

Don't let this be "just another year" of disappointing and unprofitable performance. Press in to a closer relationship with Jesus. Press through every opposing force that would hinder you. Refuse defeat, claim victory, sing His praise, fight the good fight of faith.

Make this the year of your greatest perform-ance as a Christian. Make sure that if you're tried for being a Christian, there'll be enough evidence to convict you.

Resurrection Power

> But if the Spirit of him that raised up Jesus from the dead dwell in you, he that raised up Christ from the dead shall also quicken your mortal bodies by his Spirit that dwelleth in you.
>
> ROMANS 8:11

Millions of people will put on their new Easter outfit and march off to a religious service, supposedly commemorating the resurrection of our Lord. Many of these people have no idea of what a "born again" experience is all about. While a good percentage have been introduced one way or another to the new birth, I can rejoice that I not only know Christ through the new birth, but I also know Him "in the power of His resurrection," having experienced the glorious infilling, indwelling, overflowing baptism of the Holy Spirit.

Paul writes in the above verse of the possibility of the Spirit's dwelling within, in these words: "If the Spirit of him that raised up Jesus dwell in you, he that raised up Jesus from the dead shall also *quicken* [give life, refreshing, power] to your mortal bodies by his Spirit." So there were some "saved by faith" who Paul writes to of the resurrection power of the Holy Spirit. Paul is making known a fact that is obvious to all who have received the Holy Spirit, but not known to one whom the Spirit does not indwell.

We Pentecostals will go to church this Sunday morning knowing of something that thousands know nothing of. It is this: "We have felt the power that brought Christ forth from the tomb!" While others sing, "He lives," we know of the power that enabled Him to live!

Thank God, that such poor, unworthy mortals as we, can sense and be empowered by the precious Holy Spirit while we are yet alive. This power of the Spirit has resurrected many from an obscure life and imparted His abilities, thus enabling one to do a work for Christ.

In Latin America, the evangelical believers are about 80% Pentecostal. Why? This is the reason, I believe: "The power of the Spirit." You can't cast out devils with creed and doctrine. Don't you know the devil knows those who profess their doubt by saying, "This was for the apostles only?" When a preacher says that, he is admitting that he doesn't have it (literally, the power to overthrow the devil).

Now, besides the resurrection power that accompanies the indwelling of the Holy Spirit, there is that "joy unspeakable and full of glory" experience. It is that better way of peace, joy and righteousness in the Holy Ghost.

What am I trying to say? Simply this: the baptism of the Holy Spirit is more than just speaking in other (foreign) tongues (while this is the certification that we have received Him). His presence means more than unspeakable joy. His indwelling presence in us means that we have shut up in us the power to resurrect and bring to life the ability to live a victorious life for Christ, producing the miracle of change that is so necessary for our life to be an anthem of praise unto our glorious Lord. The power to go to the ends of the earth with this Gospel. Literally, the power that brought Christ forth from the tomb. Hallelujah!

Mothers! What Is There Left To Say?

As a preacher, coming up with something interesting to say can become a heavy burden at times. So when we come to the subject of mothers, on wonders if there is anything that hasn't been said a dozen times before. Perhaps it has all been said many times, but I feel like some things are worthy of being repeated.

For instance, I believe godly mothers are as necessary for the preservation of the morals of a people s the sun is to life. Laying at the feet of thousands of women who are mothers only in the sense of giving birth to a child is the guilt and shame of this generation. The hopelessness of the young has been induced by the selfishness of mothers and fathers.

Thousands of mothers are at this moment unwitting tools of the devil, bringing about the moral decay and ruin of our society.

I believe it was President L. B. Johnson whose aim and goal was to bring to the American people a period which he terms "the Great Society." His "Great Society" became a decade of lawlessness, though he is not all to blame. You just can't have a "Great Society" without first having great mothers! Godly, praying, righteous women who instill in their children high and godly ideals.

If our nation falls—it has already fallen into moral rot and ruin—the blame will lay at the feet of passive, permissive parents who seem neither to care for or love their children. *Parents who really care for and love their children do not send them to Sunday school and church—they take them!*

Let me go a step further. Don't tell me you care about your child's future if you *make* him go to public school, but excuse his attendance in church by saying, "I don't believe in forcing them to go." You're a hypocrite if you do that! You have a double standard! But then, anyone in this position is like most of his peers anyway

———

Parents who drink and smoke often go into screaming fits of heebie-jeebies when they learn their kid is using drugs. He or she learned it from you, Mom, Dad. . . . You've been using drugs for years. That child may even have some physical weakness because you poisoned his body with nicotine and alcohol while you were carrying him, Mom. . . . So don't get so uptight if he uses a different form of drugs than you use. . . . Now, I am not condoning drugs in any form. There is deliverance in Christ!

I am saying that children follow the parents' example, and when it comes to sin, they generally exceed the example set before them.

The world needs godly mothers; the church needs godly mothers. . . . But more than any of these, *your child needs a godly mother!*

Thanksgiving Day

Giving thanks always for all things unto God and the Father in the name of our Lord Jesus Christ.

EPHESIANS 5:20

Thanksgiving Day . . . Is it enough?

To set aside a day once a year to give thanks unto God for His bountiful blessings is commendable. As we all know, it was a practice begun by our God-fearing and God-honoring forefathers; however, let us not be naive enough to believe that it was the only day they paused to give thanks, as it is with so many today.

After all, who do you think gets the most pleasure out of our Thanksgiving celebration? In most homes throughout America, there will be no mention of gratitude to God—in fact, no mention of God, period. In many others, there will be a brief table grace said in the light-hearted manner followed by the gulping of delectable foodstuffs until they finally stumble off into the den to watch a football game on TV while chewing on Rolaids to try and find some relief for their over-extended stomachs. Now, I ask you, does God get any glory out of all that?

You see, Thanksgiving is not to be a once-a-year thing. It isn't even a part-time occupation. Thanks-giving is to be a continuous experience for the Christian—an experience that produces a constant flow of gratitude unto God. And our Thanksgiving is also to be unlimited in its scope. We are to give thanks for ALL THINGS. For trial, as well as triumph; for the cross, as well as the crown; for the sickness, as well as the healing. Yes, we are to give thanks ALWAYS for ALL things unto our God and Father in the name of our Lord Jesus.

Give thanks for trial? For the cross? For sickness? Yes, for surely they must be included in all things. Can't you see that there can be no triumph without trial; there can be no crown without a cross; and there can be no healing without sickness? Yes, just go ahead and thank Him every day for all things. His eye is on the sparrow, and you can rest assured your heavenly Father is busy watching over you.

Once a year is not enough; once a day is not enough. And when we step inside those gates of pearl, we will then realize that *giving thanks always* was not enough.

Time To Be Thinkful

Finally, brethren, whatsoever things are true,
whatsoever things are honest, whatsoever things are
just, whatsoever things are pure, whatsoever things
are lovely, whatsoever things are of good report; if
there be any virtue, and if there be any praise, think
on these things.

PHILIPPIANS 4:8

The Founding Fathers of our nation were men
who gave great honor to the Bible and what the
Bible teaches. It is because of this sincere
dedication to Bible truth and a desire to express
to God the feeling of their heart and soul in
worship that we are a nation.

Now we know that they were "thankful
men," but what we sometimes fail to realize is
that they were also "thinking men." After all,
one of them *thought* of the idea of a day of
Thanksgiving and communicated his thoughts to
others who felt that this was the least that they
could do for the blessings that God had visited
them with.

Thanksgiving is a national holiday today, but
thousands make a mockery of this day. Not only
do they fail to be "thankful," but they also fail to
"think." Let me go on and say that you can't
really be "thankful" without first of all being
"thinkful."

155

So let us pause this Thanksgiving Day, and before we even attempt to thank God, let us spend some time in solemn meditation, thinking on the good, the pure, the lovely, the honest and the just things of life. Think about the times the Lord Jesus has healed you, strengthened you, and think of the peace that He constantly gives. I feel assured of this one thing, the more you are "thinkful," the more you will be "thankful." Romans 1:21 mentions those who "neither were thankful" because when they knew God, they glorified Him not as God. *They didn't think!*

Think! Think of the hope you have in Christ. Think of the hopelessness without Him. Think of all that He has prepared for His people. Think of all that the Lord is doing for people *today!* Think of all those lost in darkness, those whom the church has not reached with the Gospel, those who have no hope in this life *or* the life to come, those who know only the darkness and despair, those who cannot come to the light. And so, we must take the light to them. Think about them, and then get on your knees and give *thanks* that someone has already brought the light to you. Before you get off your knees, let's once again be "thinkful." Let us try to think of some way wherein we can do a little more to "speed the light" to those who wait in darkness.

Giving-For or For-Giving?

Give, and it shall be given unto you; good measure, pressed down, and shaken together, and running over, shall men give into your bosom. For with the same measure that ye mete withal it shall be measured to you again.

LUKE 6:38

But if ye forgive not men their trespasses, neither will your Father forgive your trespasses.

MATTHEW 6:15

This is the time of the year when almost everyone is caught up in the act of giving. However, the extent that we sometimes go to in all of this must sometimes surely be sickening to our Lord. For instance, what kind of Christianity do we have if we allow ourselves to become so involved with the commercialism of the Christmas season that we allow our spiritual life to deteriorate to the extent that we need a reviving the first thing in the new year?

Sure! It is good to be liberal, to give, to share, and there is much said in the Scriptures about giving. Even my text seems to convey the thinking of so many during this season, "Give, and it shall be given unto you" (Luke 6:38) But what Jesus is teaching is simply this: we are to give a good and honest measure; take the false

157

bottoms out of the baskets, heap it up, run it over. Jesus was speaking of giving a good measure when you sell; He was not speaking about giving for the sake of receiving something better in return.

The gifts of God are without repentance. In other words, God is never sorry about bestowing His gifts upon us. We freely receive salvation, healing and health, the Holy Ghost, and become heirs to all things.

What kind of giving can we do that would please God most? Well, I think of all the giving that we may do, "forgiving" is the most important. In fact, the Lord has made it very plain that if we do not "forgive," we cannot be forgiven ourselves.

When God gave Christ for the salvation of lost men, the act is spoken of as the "gift of God." But in this act of *giving* is also the act of FORGIVING, for our pardon and forgiveness is what Christ came to accomplish. Why not follow the example of our Lord this Christmas season? Do something wonderful for yourself and for those around you: FORGIVE, and then live in the sweet peace of that forgiveness throughout the coming year. It will be the greatest gift that you can give, with certainly the greatest reward.

There Really Is a Santa Claus!

Some of you are smiling and saying to yourself, "what's the pastor up to now?" Now, why do you find it so difficult to believe in a Santa Claus when there are thousands of people that do? Why, sure, while they may not believe in a jolly giant with reindeer and sled who spreads cheer and leaves gifts in every home, they believe in something just as mythical or ridiculous. For instance, there are thousands who believe that somehow they're going to wind up in heaven when they die, even though they have ignored God and His Christ, His Church, His messengers and His Word. Anybody who can believe that shouldn't have the least bit of trouble believing in a Santa Claus.

And take the Jehovah's Witness crowd, who would be a star attraction in any circus for their juggling act if they could juggle other things like they can the Scripture. Anyone that can profess to believe the Bible as they do and then fail to see the Sonship and deity of Jesus Christ; anyone that can read the Bible and fail to believe in a literal burning place of torment called hell; anyone that can be that ignorant and naive, can and must believe in a Santa Claus.

And take the messageless Mormons, whose closest resemblance to New Testament Christianity is that they go two by two. Why, anyone who can believe the verbal espousings of a Joseph Smith—whose history points to a questionable life—over the inspired, God-breathed Word of God, surely must not find the mind-boggling myth of a Santa Claus too difficult to accept.

Now, if I accept much of the teaching in the world today, I would have to believe in Santa Claus. But since I refuse to believe anything else but the Word of God and that Jesus is the Way, the Truth and the Life, and there is no other name given under heaven whereby men may be saved, and since I believe that "glory, honor and peace" come to the man that *does good*, and "anguish, tribulation, wrath and indignation" come upon the soul of a man that does evil (Rom. 2:9-10), I really can't believe in a Santa Claus.

My friend, quit living in a dream world filled with mythical nonsense. Face up to the facts! If you haven't accepted Christ as Lord and Savior, then you are headed and are going to eternal hell unless you repent. If you are a Christian, rejoice in your salvation, follow Christ—if you don't know how, read the Gospel—live for Him, and keep yourself in the love of God (Jude 21). Quit believing in Santa Claus! You're not going to heaven unless you have been truly born again and are living a victorious, overcoming life in Jesus Christ.

"This Is Your Life"

A thank-you letter written on the occasion of a celebration of Pastor Hill's legacy in Wichita, Kansas.

First of all, to those will read this that weren't privileged to be present on Homecoming Day, November 4th, 1973, let me clue you in on what happened.

For several weeks, a handful of workers had been secretly working to provide me with the surprise of a lifetime. Now, preachers have a lot of memorable experiences, but believe me when I say that this day was an unforgettable experience; so overwhelming, that now, three days later, as I write this, I am still in somewhat of a daze.

These workers had quietly and secretly brought into the city . . . my three sisters; three of my nieces; my mother-in-law and father-in-law; my wife's sister; my General Superintendent; the Director of World Missions; my District Superintendent and his parents; Bro.

and Sis. Sanson and daughter, former District Superintendent of ours and dear friends; Bible School students from our church that I thought were in school in Houston; Sis. Guines and son, Larry, former members of the church I pastored in Houston—and there were others. All of this for a presentation beautifully carried out, entitled "Fred A. Hill, Jr.—This Is Your Life."

Many have asked about my reactions, my feelings, my thoughts, as the program began to unfold. Well, first, let me say that I was prepared to preach, planning to conserve time in order to give Sis. Higbee the ten minutes at the close for what I thought to be a presentation from the Pirates' Den, but this is what happened:

Bro. McCormick enters with Dr. Heard and proceeds to the pulpit. When I saw them coming, I was thrilled to think that the church had surprised me by bringing in the General Superintendent to minister to us today! But a few seconds later, I knew that was something different about all this. Then I heard the words: "Fred A. Hill, Jr. This is your life," followed by a few remarks concerning my birth and childhood. And then, suddenly, my oldest sister's voice broke from the balcony. My first thoughts were, they have gotten a recording from her—but, no, here Gladys comes down the aisle and presents me with a poem I had written at about the age of eleven. Well, this starts the shockwaves, and my mind goes into a whir of flashbacks of days gone by: the old sawmill, happy days on the farm, my brother hauling wood, an innocent little nephew named Glen who sits for a few minutes on a box in the corner of the room, convinced by my mischievous father that he really could lay an egg . . . A letter from Rex Humbard was read—I was saved under the Humbard family's ministry over 25 years ago.

Then the voice of a niece—I thought it was Shirley's voice, but, no, it was Becky. Could she be here? Yes, she was. Next, the voice of my sister, Marjorie. Could all this be true?

Then, a familiar voice rang out in song—my sister, Tiny's. She can't be here, but she is . . . This is too much! How did they manage this impossible feat?

Letters from Dean Elizabeth Williams and Mrs. S. D. Doyle, dear friends who remember former days before I was married to Miss Betty Jane Kiff. No mistaking these next voices—Bro. and Sis. Kiff, my mother-in-law and father-in-law—two of the most wonderful people on earth —they're here too! Then the voice and entrance of Sis. Thornton, "Boojie," my sister-in-law, a real pest when Sis. Hill and I were courting.

Then Betty Zane Nesbit, reminding me of the first wedding over 17 years ago . . . Bro. and Sis. Bernard, true and dear friends, who were such a blessing to us when we were so in need . . . Bro and Sis. Sanson and Regina, my Superintendent for years—fishing buddy, true friends, so close, we feel like they're members of our family.

Another familiar voice, and this time I am right; it is Shirley, my niece, who, along with her sister, remembered some things I can't recall.

I am, by this time, so overwhelmed and in such a state of shock that I can't recall very well my reaction and surprise to the presence of the others. But Bro. Bob Boyle, you told me you couldn't be here; but you're forgiven. Sis. Guynes and Larry, what a long way to drive, but I am so glad you did.

Bro. Don Shute, I enjoyed working with you so close those two years; God help us both to never slacken our pace for world evangelism.

Bro. Art Hazen, God bless you, dear brother, for representing those who were with us in all the remodelling—so many memories as we look over the church and think of those who so faithfully labored for the Lord.

Sis. Newman—the first convert from our ministry here—God bless you—God's grace is marvelous; the blood never loses its power.

Bro. and Sis. Boyle, Sr. and Ivan, it was such a delight to have you with us; and Ivan, faithful radio listener and dear brother in Christ. His blessings be upon you.

Larry Graham—former assistant, District PYPA President—a real leader—destined to be a bachelor.

College kids—Mike Jayne, Betty Westerfield, Pam Lothes, Sherri Taylor—what a surprise! God bless you, and I love you.

Bro. Bill Hamby, your words of kindness, it's too much! Bless you!

All of this is interspersed with congratulatory letters and telegrams from friends and associates from Congressman Shriver, Governor Docking, U. S. Senator Dole, and finally one signed—no, this can't be—but yes, it is—a greeting from the president, Richard Nixon! Please, I can't take much more . . . This is just too much!

My normal reaction to a joyous moment is to laugh, not weep, but the joy of this hour was too much—too overwhelming. Mixed emotions began to flood my heart. Feelings of pride and humility. Proud that my congregation thought this much of me, and at the same moment, terribly humbled by the tremendous demonstration of love manifested by our congregation and those who came from so far away to be present on this day. And wasn't the meal lovely, and please, if I seemed to be in a daze—I was. Please forgive me if I, in any way, seemed to be unfriendly or ungrateful. The shock of the occasion was almost too much for me.

Thank you, congregation, for an unforgettable morning, November 4th, 1973.

To Sis. Higbee, who bore the responsibility of planning all this, assisted by Bro. Higbee, Bro. and Sis. McCormick, Bro and Sis. John Fry, Sis. Westerfield, Sis. Hoppins, Sis. Moss and Bro. Max—my sincere thanks for a day never to be forgotten.

To all the other committees, who worked so hard to ready the church building, and prepared the meal, the decorations, the arrangements, etc. —you are tremendous! *No* pastor has a greater congregation than I.

And to my faithful and loving wife, Betty, who keeps a secret so well, and who never ceases to encourage and challenge me to a greater ministry in Christ—thanks, Honey!

To my children, Kevan and Suzzette—thank you for all your help in Daddy's ministry. Your playing and singing was beautiful.

To my wonderful Lord, whose call still throbs in my heart . . . Thank you, Lord, for blessing me far beyond measure. I'm unworthy, but thankful.

TRIBULATION SURVIVAL
INSTRUCTIONS

What To Do If You Are Left Behind

All Scripture quotations in this section are from the NIV translation.

The rapture has come and you are left behind. **You have missed the rapture!**

The events of the last few hours leave you bewildered, shocked, and confused. Millions have suddenly disappeared, leaving behind havoc, destruction and death. The freeways are jammed with wrecks caused by suddenly driverless autos; airliners have crashed because of disappearing pilots; and on the television, somber, ashen-faced newspeople relate accounts of death, destruction, and mysterious disappearances. They refer to one thing as a possible explanation—***the rapture.***

What, precisely, has happened? Briefly, this: the rapture as taught in the Bible was a sudden, unannounced catching away of all the dead in Christ and all the living in Christ. According to

Scripture, these people were changed to immortality and went to meet the Lord Jesus Christ in the air, to be forever with Him. For years Bible-believing churches have taught the fact of the rapture, warning repeatedly that it was going to come. As many as would listen have been alerted concerning the signs and developments pointing to the event.

> For the Lord himself will come down from heaven, with a loud command, with the voice of the archangel and with the trumpet call of God, and the dead in Christ will rise first. After that, we who are still alive and are left will be caught up with them in the clouds to meet the Lord in the air. And so we will be with the Lord forever.
>
> 1 THESSALONIANS 4:16-17

> Listen, I will tell you a mystery. We shall not all sleep [i.e., die], but we shall all be changed—in a flash, in the twinkling of an eye, at the last trumpet. For the trumpet will sound, the dead will be raised imperishable, and we shall be changed."
>
> 1 CORINTHIANS 15:51, 52

So, my friend, this is briefly what has taken place. We, the church—those in Christ—are gone and you, along with millions of others, are left behind to face an unknown fate.

But wait … THERE IS HOPE! There is the possibility of survival! I speak of survival in the sense of the **survival** or **salvation** of your **soul.**

Choosing salvation for your soul will mean that you, no doubt, will lose your physical life as a martyr for Christ. The possibility of such survival depends upon your following the instructions I have outlined for you in this book. **Every detail must be attended to with the utmost care.** The instructions follow:

FIRST!

Your survival depends entirely upon your **committing your life now to Jesus Christ.** Do not hesitate; do it now! Do it now while the impact of what has happened is fresh in your mind and before the lying spirits from hell have flooded the earth.

> The coming of the lawless one [the Antichrist] will be in accordance with the work of Satan displayed in all kinds of counterfeit miracles, signs and wonders, and in every sort of evil that deceives those who are perishing. They perish because they refused to love the truth and so be saved. For this reason God sends them a powerful delusion so that they will believe the lie.
>
> 2 THESSALONIANS 2:9-11

If you do not know how to pray, then pray this prayer:

"Heavenly Father, I confess that I have sinned against You and against Your Son, the Lord Jesus Christ. I have ignored the warnings that were given by Your minister's Father, and now I find myself left behind, facing an unknown fate. I throw myself entirely upon Your mercy. Heavenly Father, forgive me in the name of Jesus! I take You, Jesus, as my Lord and Savior. I will confess you before others. I will trust You. By faith, I thank you for saving me!"

After you have surrendered and committed your life and future to the Lordship of Jesus Christ, **begin immediately to share this** with others—your family members, relatives, and neighbors. **Form small cell groups and begin to make preparations for the most difficult time in human history. Cell groups are vital because there is strength in unity,** and you will need all the strength and help you can get. The road ahead will not be easy, but you are now a desperate individual in desperate, seemingly hopeless circumstances.

SECOND!

One of the things you may face is an overwhelming urge to take your own life, due to the apparent hopelessness of the present situation.

Again, let me remind you, this is the work of the lying spirits that will flood the earth with this and other delusions. You must resist suicide with everything in your power. You will hear of thousands committing suicide, but your survival depends upon your resisting this Satanic impulse. You must prepare to lose your life for Jesus Christ, but you **must not take your own life.** To do so is to once and for all seal your destiny for hell.

THIRD!

If you are a member of a church, remember that your church did not meet your need and prepare you for the rapture! Realize now that you are all alone. Your church may still have its doors open but it does not have the answers and the help you need! **Believe what I say and you will survive and help others to survive. Reject these instructions and you reject your only way out!**

> The Spirit clearly says that in later times some will abandon the faith and follow deceiving spirits and things taught by demons.
>
> 1 TIMOTHY 4:1

> While evil men and impostors will go from bad to worse, deceiving and being deceived.
>
> 2 TIMOTHY 3:13

> First of all, you must understand that in the last days scoffers will come, scoffing and following their

own evil desires. They will say, "Where is this 'coming' he promised?"

2 PETER 3:3-4

These scriptures should make it crystal clear that what I am saying to you is truth. **If your church did not teach you about repentance, the new birth, and the rapture, it failed you miser-ably.** But bitterness toward them will not help you now. **You must forgive them and with these instructions help them to genuinely find Jesus Christ and survive the tribulation.**

FOURTH!

Get your Bible off the shelf. If you don't have a Bible, we believers have left numbers of them behind in our homes, churches, and bookstores; **you are welcome to them!** Begin immediately to **commit the Scripture to memory**, especially the New Testament. You are facing a STORM SURGE of Satanic delusion and power! Your Bible and related materials—such as this book—will possibly be taken from you. You must prepare for this by committing the Scripture to memory so that you will always have a portion of the word of God in your heart. Jesus said, **"Heaven and earth will pass away, but my words will never pass away" (Matthew 24:35).** The Word of God

172

that has provided strength and comfort to believers before the rapture will do the same for you now!

FIFTH!

Two major changes that will produce dramatic, catastrophic events are imminent. **The first is a change in God's attitude!** His mercy and love will give way to judgment and wrath.

> Then the kings of the earth, the princes, the generals, the rich, the mighty, and every slave and every free man hid in caves and among the rocks of the mountains. They called to the mountains and the rocks, 'Fall on us and hide us from the face of him who sits on the throne and from the wrath of the Lamb! For the great day of their [the Father's and the Son's] wrath has come, and who can stand?
>
> REVELATION 6:15-17

For 6,000 years God has dealt tenderly and compassionately with man. Since the flood in Noah's day (4,000 years ago) God has dealt in mercy and grace, while judgment upon men has been localized and limited. You lived in the grace period before the rapture, so you may be aware of His unmerited favor or grace. His grace will still be extended to you if you ask for it, but the pleading, loving tenderness in which God dealt with men in the past will not be the situation now. The world's cup of wickedness—

173

sin against God—is full, and **God will now move from mercy and grace to wrath** for the next seven years. So I give you warning! If you live in a city that promotes and pushes alternate lifestyles while rejecting and punishing Biblical lifestyles—**MOVE!** God's hatred for homosexual behavior is plainly spelled out in the Bible. He is totally intolerant of such sin and, now that His attitude of grace is changing, I am certain that these cities will be destroyed as Sodom and Gomorrah were destroyed.

Another reason **you will need to move** from such an area is that individuals who give themselves to such lusts have receptive minds and bodies through which Satan is working. They will rise up in opposition to you or anyone else who will try to live for Jesus Christ. You will have difficulty enough without staying around where **you will be an open target** for Satanic attack **through delusion, subtlety, or outright coercion!** I know that even before we left in the rapture, people were openly declaring their alternate lifestyles and their rage against any Christian opposition, though deviant physical coercion and rape were not widespread. Now that the influence of Jesus Christ through his body—the Church—is gone, such godless activity will most certainly increase.

You will not be able to hide the fact that you are a Christian (no one could ever truly do that), but it is only exercising wisdom, especially at this time, to live in an area that will minimize the difficulties.

The **second major change** will be a dramatic increase in **Satanic activity in the earth.**

> Therefore rejoice, you heavens and you who dwell in them! But woe to the earth and the sea, because the devil has gone down to you! He is filled with fury, because he knows that his time is short."
>
> REVELATION 12:12

This increase in **Satanic activity** will result in increased sexual perversion and the rise of Satanic cults, false religions, and witchcraft. There will be increased murder, rape, brutality, crimes of passion, and inhumanity to others, plus the following seven significant international events:

(5.1) War on Israel.

> So when you see standing in the Holy Place "the abomination that causes desolation," spoken of through the prophet Daniel—let the reader understand—then let those who are in Judea flee to the mountains. Let no man on the roof of his house go down to take anything out of the house. Let no one in the field go back to get his cloak. How dreadful it will be in those days for pregnant women and nursing mothers! Pray that your flight

will not take place in the winter or on the Sabbath. For then there will be great distress, unequaled from the beginning of the world until now, and never to be equaled again.

MATTHEW 24:15-21

(5.2) Forced Worship of Satan and the Antichrist.

Men worshipped the Dragon because he had given authority to the beast, and they also worshipped the beast and asked, 'Who is like the beast? Who can make war against him?' The beast was given a mouth to utter proud words and blasphemies and to exercise his authority for forty-two months. He opened his mouth to blaspheme God, and to slander his name and his dwelling place and those who live in heaven. He was given power to make war against the saints and conquer them. And he was given authority over every tribe, people, language and nation. All inhabitants of the earth will worship the beast—all whose names have not been written in the book of life belonging to the Lamb that was slain from the creation of the world. He who has an ear, let him hear. If anyone is to go into captivity, into captivity he will go. If anyone is to be killed with the sword, with the sword he will be killed. This calls for patient endurance and faithfulness on the part of the saints.

REVELATION 13:4-10

(5.3) Deception by Miracles.

And he performed great and miraculous signs, even causing fire to come down from heaven to earth in full view of men. Because of the signs he was given power to do on behalf of the first beast, he deceived the inhabitants of the earth. He ordered them to set up an image in honor of the beast who was wounded by the sword and yet lived. He was given power to give breath to the image of the first beast, so that it could speak and cause all who refused to worship the image to be killed.

REVELATION 13:13-15

For false Christs and false prophets will appear and perform great signs and miracles to deceive even the elect—if that were possible.

MATTHEW 24:24

(5.4) Physical Mark to Buy or Sell.

He also forced everyone, small and great, rich and poor, free and slave, to receive a mark on his right hand or on his forehead, so that no one could buy or sell unless he had the mark, which is the name of the beast or the number of his name.

REVELATION 13:16

(5.5) Forced Denial of God.

He was given power to make war against the saints and to conquer them. And he was given authority over every tribe, people, language and nation.

REVELATION 13:7

(5.6) World Wars.

At the time of the end the king of the South will engage him in battle, and the king of the North [Antichrist] will storm out against him with chariots and cavalry and a great fleet of ships. He will invade many countries and sweep through them like a flood.

DANIEL 11:40

(5.7) Mobilization of Nations.

Then they gathered the Kings together to the place that in Hebrew is called "Armageddon."

REVELATION 16:16

I saw heaven standing open and there before me was a white horse, whose rider is called Faithful and True. With justice he judges and makes war. His eyes are like blazing fire, and on his head are many crowns. He has a name written on him that no one knows but he himself. He is dressed in a robe dipped in blood, and his name is the Word of God. The armies of heaven were following him, riding on white horses and dressed in fine linen, white and clean. Out of his mouth comes a sharp sword with which to strike down the nations. "He will rule them with an iron scepter." He treads the winepress of the fury of the wrath of God Almighty. On his robe and on his thigh he has this name written: KING OF KINGS AND LORD OF LORDS.

And I saw an angel standing in the sun, who cried in a loud voice to all the birds flying in midair,

178

"Come gather together for the great supper of God, so that you may eat the flesh of kings, generals, and mighty men, of horses and their riders, and the flesh of all people, free and slave, small and great." Then I saw the beast and the kings of the earth and their armies gathered together to make war against the rider on the horse and his army. But the beast was captured and with him the false prophet who had performed the miraculous signs on his behalf. With these signs he had deluded those who had received the mark of the beast and worshiped his image. The two of them were thrown alive into the fiery lake of burning sulfur. The rest of them were killed with the sword that came out of the mouth of the rider on the horse, and all the birds gorged themselves on their flesh.

REVELATION 19:11-21

SIXTH!

Dramatic changes in government, business and society will shortly come to pass! **Because of the great number of people missing from the earth** (and especially so among some Western nations), **confusion reigns**. Key personnel in the military and in the government—federal, state and local—are missing. Key personnel in manufacturing, banking, and the construction business are gone. **The most reliable element of the entire social structure has disappeared from**

the earth. Weary, confused government officials plead for calm. **Looting and lawlessness prevail everywhere. Martial law will soon be in effect** as the only means available to cope with the lawlessness. Do not participate in lawless activity. Be wise, yet help one another (especially fellow new Christians) with the basic needs of life—safety, food, shelter and truth about Christ.

All these perplexing social problems are compounded by earthquakes, floods, and dramatic changes in weather patterns. It seems the **whole planet is in the throes of rebellion and death. You need one another's help!**

SEVENTH!

Keep your eyes upon what happens to Israel—it is vital to your survival that you do so and recognize the following as it happens. An announcement will come at any time that Israel has signed a seven-year **covenant of peace** with a king or ruler of great influence and power. There are **four important things** to recognize **about the ruler:**

(1) He will be from a country north of Israel (Daniel 11:40-45).

(2) He will begin making war with other nations in that part of the world, the oil-rich nations and the area around the Mediterranean

Sea. He will be successful in conquering and dominating a part of this area.

(3) He will break his covenant with Israel in three-and-a-half years (Daniel 9:27). Some may have already been killed for their faith in Jesus by this time.

(4) He is the Antichrist; it is vital that you remember this!

EIGHTH!

Do not worship anyone except the Lord Jesus Christ! Do not worship any image or likeness of anyone!

The mysterious and miraculous will be almost commonplace. Images of the Antichrist will actually take on life from demonic power, to the extent that they will speak and cause men who will not worship the images to be killed (Revelation 13:15).

Do not take any kind of physical mark, visible or invisible, that has anything to do with this ruler. It would be best not to take any mark at all.

God has already pronounced eternal damnation on anyone who worships the Antichrist or his image, or who takes his mark (Revelation 14:9-11).

Some of you may find yourself in the position of either losing your job (because of foreign trade, the oil business, or a government position) or being forced to comply with this ruler whom we call the Antichrist. Whatever it costs you personally—even your life—do not have anything at all to do with this ruler or his government. Do not support him in any way. If you are in the military and you are assigned to a unit that will join his war effort, desert! (I would not normally advocate desertion, but in this situation it is absolutely necessary.)

NINTH!

Famine—always a stark reality in much of the world—it **is now rapidly becoming worldwide**. War—looting—burning—pilfering —destruction has depleted the food reserves and the war machine has ruthlessly destroyed the grain and vegetable fields, plus the fact that farmers have been called into military service.

In the U.S., thousands of farms lie idle— crops unharvested, fields growing up in weeds, stock dying from lack of care, machinery idle. The world's bread basket lacks the personnel to farm and produce, too many people are missing —gone in the rapture.

Shortages exist everywhere. The need to grow and process your own food is vital. You must **adjust to a much different standard of living than what you had before.**

TENTH!

Do not get caught up in the false hopes of the world around you. Your only hope is in God!!

Do not be lulled into believing that things are going to get better ... that God, after all, did us a favor in taking His people out because there were too many people anyway ... that now, after a brief period of adjustment, everything will really be better and there will be more than enough food and energy for everyone. This is a Satanic delusion, a deception, a lie!

Prepare to lay down your life! There is absolutely no hope for this world! Do what you can to sustain yourself as long as you can do it honestly, before God. **Do not steal, cheat, lie or bear false witness. Do forgive all those who offend or harm you, even your executioner!**

END-TIME EVENTS

I have catalogued the major tribulation period events of the Book of Revelation in the following pages. This has been done so that you may have firsthand knowledge of these things as you see them develop. (Remember, some events may seem to occur simultaneously and others may appear to not be sequential. Some events may be noticed before they reach their fullness or height of severity.)

It is a catalogue of terror! The next seven years will entail one incredibly horrifying experience after another, consummating in the greatest battle of all time—**the Battle of Armageddon**.

These horrors will begin with the rise of an ambitious conqueror, whom the Bible defines as the Antichrist.

> I watched as the Lamb opened the first of the seven seals. Then I heard one of the four living creatures say in a voice like thunder, "Come!" I looked, and there before me was a white horse! Its rider held a bow, and he was given a crown, and he rode out as a conqueror bent on conquest.
>
> REVELATION 6:1-2

This man will begin to war with the nations of the Middle East and the nations around the Mediterranean, as I stated previously. These wars, coupled with other strange and unusual events, will result in death and destruction as nothing else ever has.

Following the wars, famines, pestilence, death and hell on earth—the result of the wrath of man—will be the beginning of the wrath of God.

(1) First, there will be hail and fire mingled with blood. This rain at first will cause 33% of the trees and all the green grass to be burned up.

> The first angel sounded his trumpet, and there came hail and fire mixed with blood, and it was hurled down upon the earth. A third of the earth was burned up, a third of the trees were burned up, and all the green grass was burned up.
>
> REVELATION 8:7

(2) Second, one third of the sea will become blood, a third of the creatures of the sea will die, and a third of the ships will be destroyed.

> The second angel sounded his trumpet, and something like a huge mountain, all ablaze, was thrown into the sea. A third of the sea turned into blood, a third of the living creatures in the sea died, and a third of the ships were destroyed.
>
> REVELATION 8:8-9

(3) Third, one-third of the rivers and springs become Wormwood (poisoned) and many people will die because of the poisoning of the water.

> The third angel sounded his trumpet, and a great star, blazing like a torch, fell from the sky on a third of the rivers and on the springs of water—the name of the star is Wormwood. A third of the water turned bitter, and many people died from the waters that had become bitter.
>
> REVELATION 8:10-11

(4) Fourth, darkness will prevail; goodbye solar power and solar heat! The earth will begin to cool down and vegetation will begin to die. Frozen in fear, men—for the most part—will go unrepentant as God smites the sun, moon, and stars until their light is reduced by one-third.

> The fourth angel sounded his trumpet, and a third of the sun was struck, a third of the moon, and a third of the stars, so that a third of them turned dark. A third of the day was without light, and also a third of the night.
>
> REVELATION 8:12

(5) Fifth, further darkening of the sun and pollution of the air will occur as the bottomless pit is opened and smoke arises from the abyss as a great furnace. But more than smoke comes forth; demons are loosed upon men, demons shaped to a locust but with tails like scorpions. They will torment men for five months; and so great will be his torment that man will seek to destroy himself. But there will be no way of escape, for a period of five months there will be no death on this planet.

> The fifth angel sounded his trumpet, and I saw a star that had fallen from the sky to the earth. The star was given the key to the shaft of the Abyss. When he opened the Abyss, smoke rose from it like the smoke from a gigantic furnace. The sun and sky were darkened by the smoke from the Abyss. And

out of the smoke locusts came down on the earth and were given power like that of scorpions of the earth. They were told not to harm the grass of the earth or any plant or tree, but only those who did not have the seal of God on their foreheads. They were not given power to kill them, but only to torture them for five months. And the agony they suffered was like the sting of a scorpion when it strikes a man. During those days, men will seek death, but will not find it; they will long to die, but death will elude them.

REVELATION 9:1-6

But wait… there is more.

(6) Sixth, many of those who earlier wished to die will now have the opportunity; in fact **one third** of all who live upon the earth will be killed by fire, smoke, or brimstone. Yet there will be no wholesale or mass repentance among men.

The sixth angel blew his trumpet, and I heard a voice coming from the horns of the golden altar that is before God. It said to the sixth angel who had the trumpet, "Release the four angels who are bound at the great river Euphrates." And the four angels who had been kept ready for this very hour and day and month and year were released to kill a third of mankind. The number of mounted troops was two hundred million. I heard the number.
The horses and riders I saw in my vision looked like this: Their breastplates were fiery red, dark blue,

187

and yellow as sulfur. A third of mankind was killed by the three plagues of fire, smoke and sulfur that came out of their mouths. The power of the horses was in their mouths and in their tails; for their tails were like snakes, having heads with which they inflict injury.

The rest of mankind that were not killed by these plagues still did not repent of the work of their hands; they did not stop worshipping demons, and idols of gold, silver, bronze, stone and wood—idols that cannot see or hear or walk. Nor did they repent of their murders, their magic arts, their sexual immorality or their thefts.

REVELATION 9:13-21

Now my friend, if you think the horrors we have previously mentioned are incredible, unbelievable, let me tell you that they are not over. In fact, these devastating events will continue to take place in the next three-and-a-half years. **Regretfully and horror of horrors, the worst is yet to come!**

(7) **After three-and-a-half years, the covenant of peace made by the Antichrist with Israel will be broken**—first by his armies marching into Israeli territory, and second by his polluting the temple of the Jews with his pagan practices, which are detestable to the Jews.

(8) Next, watch for two strangely dressed men who will be prophets of God with great power. They will be in Jerusalem, so the news media should carry their actions and their messages as they prophesy of future events. They will wear sackcloth (coarse cloth), a symbol of mourning. These two prophets will stop the rain, turn water to blood and smite the earth with other plagues as often as they choose, for God has given them this power.

And I will give power to my two witnesses, and they will prophesy for 1,260 days, clothed in sackcloth. These are the two olive trees and the two lampstands that stand before the Lord of the earth. If anyone tries to harm them, fire comes from their mouths and devours their enemies. This is how anyone who wants to harm them must die. These men have power to shut up the sky so that it will not rain during the time they are prophesying; and they have power to turn the waters into blood and to strike the earth with every kind of plague as often as they want.

Now when they have finished their testimony, the beast that comes up from the Abyss will attack them, and overpower and kill them. Their bodies will lie in the street of the great city, which is figuratively called Sodom and Egypt, where also their Lord was crucified. For three and a half days men from every people, tribe, and language and nation will gaze on their bodies and refuse them burial. The inhabitants of the earth will gloat over them and will celebrate by sending each other gifts, because these two prophets had tormented those who live on the earth.

But after the three and a half days a breath of life from God entered them, and they stood on their feet, and terror struck those who saw them. Then they heard a loud voice from heaven saying to them, "Come up here." And they went up to heaven in a cloud, while their enemies looked on.

At that very hour there was a severe earthquake and a tenth of the city collapsed. Seven thousand people were killed in the earthquake, and the survivors were terrified and gave glory to the God of heaven.

REVELATION 11:3-13

These two witnesses will prophesy and do miracles for three-and-a-half years. Do not speak against them, for they are God's men! He will raise them from the dead and visibly take them to heaven while the world watches!

(10) During this time men will be afflicted with a **plague of painful boils or sores**. Keep in mind that these things are the judgment of God upon men for their wicked deeds and **no medication will rid men of them**.

(11) While one third of the sea became blood in the first three and a half years, now **all the sea becomes blood** and the rivers and springs become blood. Why? Why? Why? This is why! Men have been guilty of killing (spilling the blood of) the prophets and saints of God; so, in judgment, God will give them blood to drink.

> For they have shed the blood of your holy people and your prophets, and you have given them blood to drink as they deserve.

(12) Soon the sun, moon and stars will lose one-third of their life-sustaining light, but later on—in the last three-and-a-half years—**the sun will become so bright and hot that men will actually be scorched by it.**

The heat will be so great that air conditioners will be ineffective, yet man will still blaspheme God rather than repent.

(13) Now, men who have cursed the heat and the light will suddenly be **thrown into darkness**—from fiery, piercing, blinding brightness and heat to impenetrable darkness. This is a **darkness so heavy and so great that men will gnaw their tongues in pain and horror** of what might come next!

> The first angel went and poured out his bowl on the land, and ugly and painful sores broke out on the people who had the mark of the beast and worshipped his image. The second angel poured out his bowl on the sea, and it turned into blood like that of a dead man, and every living thing in the sea died.

The third angel poured out his bowl on the rivers and springs of water, and they became blood. Then I heard the angel in charge of the waters say: "You are just in these judgments, you who are and were, the Holy One, because you have so judged; for they have shed the blood of your saints and prophets, and you have given them blood to drink as they deserve." And I heard the altar respond: "Yes, Lord God Almighty, true and just are your judgments."

The fourth angel poured out his bowl on the sun, and the sun was given power to scorch people with fire. They were seared by the intense heat and they cursed the name of God, who had control over these plagues, but they refused to repent and glorify him.

The fifth angel poured out his bowl on the throne of the beast, and his kingdom was plagued into darkness. Men gnawed their tongues in agony and cursed the God of heaven because of their pains and their sores, but they refused to repent of what they had done.

REVELATION 16:2-11

If you have accepted Jesus Christ as your personal Savior, it is doubtful that you will still be alive after the first three and a half years of horrors. **You are possibly headed for martyrdom for your testimony; that is the key to the strategy of survival. Prepare to die for Jesus so that you might gain life eternal.** You see, the world in which you are left will begin to see a deluge of demons,

not all visible, but all with one goal in mind—
that is, to keep you from becoming a Christian
who is willing to die for the faith. They will
endeavor to prevent the fulfillment of God's plan
on the earth.

Through the influence of demons, govern-
ments from all over the world will **send their
armies and commit their resources to do
battle—against Israel,** they think, but it is
actually against Jesus Christ. **The river
Euphrates will be dried up to make way
for the hordes from the east. The Battle
of Armageddon is about to take place.**

"Therefore rejoice, you heavens and you who dwell
in them! But woe to the earth and the sea, because
the devil has gone down to you! He is filled with
fury, because he knows that his time is short."

When the dragon saw that he had been hurled to
the earth, he pursued the woman who had given
birth to the male child. The woman was given two
wings of a great eagle, so that she might fly to the
place prepared for her in the desert, where she
would be taken care of for a time, times and half a
time, out of the serpent's reach. Then from his
mouth the serpent spewed water like a river, to
overtake the woman and sweep her away from the
torrent. But the earth helped the woman by
opening its mouth and swallowing the river that the
dragon had spewed out of his mouth.

REVELATION 12:12-16

The world by this time has been bombed by meteors, has suffered through numerous wars, famines, and pestilences, and has seen one third of the population die by demonic attack. Many have themselves sought death because the sting of a locust-like creature, suffered through the chill of a partially obscured sun and moon, experienced devastating hail, fire and brimstone, cried out in horror of only having blood to drink or poisoned water, sweltered in the blistering heat of a scorching sun, and gnawed their tongues under the plague of agonizing darkness, yet there still remain three horrible experiences.

(14) The greatest earthquake since man has been upon earth will take place! Jerusalem is divided into three parts by this quake. If not earlier, most certainly at this time, the cities which have promoted homosexuality, Satanic cults and other perversions will be destroyed by this shaking. Major cities of the nations will fall. Islands of the sea will disappear, mountains are leveled. Usually earth-quakes are localized, but this is a worldwide shaking, as though the earth is in its death throes.

(15) These earthquakes will be followed by or coupled with **the rain of hailstones weighing from 56 to 114 pounds**. Can you imagine the devastation the earth will feel from this?

Then there came flashes of lightning, rumblings, peals of thunder and a severe earthquake. No earthquake like it has ever occurred since man has been on earth, so tremendous was the quake. The great city split into three parts, and the cities of the nations collapsed. God remembered Babylon the Great and gave her the cup filled with the wine of the fury of his wrath. Every island fled away and the mountains could not be found. From the sky huge hailstones of about a hundred pounds each fell upon men. And they cursed God on account of the plague of hail, because the plague was so terrible.

REVELATION 16:18-21

(16) The armies are now gathered in the Valley of Megiddo, numbering in the millions. The above mentioned earthquake and hail could happen while they are assembled there. They are awaiting word from their commander-in-chief, the Antichrist. The word comes to "move out" and then **suddenly a light appears, a light brighter than noonday sun. It is Jesus Christ!** The heavenly balcony is filled with myriads of saints on white horses, a word (a sword) comes out of His mouth and it is all over. The river of blood reaches to the height of a horse's bridle for approximately 200 miles—an indescribably horrible scene. One is simply not able to comprehend it all.

They were trampled in the winepress outside the city, and blood flowed out of the press, rising as high as the horses' bridles for a distance of 1,600 stadia.

REVELATION 14:20

Then I saw the beast and the kings of the earth and their armies gathered together to make war against the rider on the horse and his army. But the beast was captured, and with him the false prophet who had performed the miraculous signs on his behalf. With these signs he had deluded those who had received the mark of the beast and worshiped his image. The two of them were thrown alive into the fiery lake of burning sulfur. The rest of them were killed with the sword that came out of the mouth of the rider on the horse, and all the birds gorged themselves on their flesh.

REVELATION 18:19-21

I have briefly detailed these judgments that will be breaking forth upon the earth, giving Scriptural documentation, so that you will be able to see and understand what is happening and also to give credibility to what I have left you in this book.

If you **adhere** to these detailed instructions, **I will see you in heaven! If you do not . . . we will never meet.**

Made in the USA
San Bernardino, CA
15 April 2018